LEARNING RESOURCES CTR/NEW ENGLAND TECH.
GEN   BF463.M4 D65 1986

P9-CTQ-634

NEW ENGLAND INSTITUTE
OF TECHNOLOGY
LEARNING RESOURCES CENTER

BF 463 .M4 D65 1986

Donaldson, Morag L.

Children's explanations

DATE DUE

MAR 2 1 1998			

DEMCO 38-297

Children's explanations

Children's explanations
A psycholinguistic study

Morag L. Donaldson

Department of Psychology, Plymouth Polytechnic

NEW ENGLAND INSTITUTE
OF TECHNOLOGY
LEARNING RESOURCES CENTER

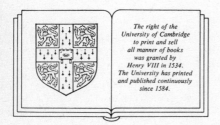

*The right of the
University of Cambridge
to print and sell
all manner of books
was granted by
Henry VIII in 1534.
The University has printed
and published continuously
since 1584.*

Cambridge University Press

Cambridge

London   New York   New Rochelle

Melbourne   Sydney

13270387

Published by the Press Syndicate of the University of Cambridge
The Pitt Building, Trumpington Street, Cambridge CB2 1RP
32 East 57th Street, New York, NY 10022, USA
10 Stamford Road, Oakleigh, Melbourne 3166, Australia

© Cambridge University Press 1986

First published 1986

Printed in Great Britain by the University Press, Cambridge

British Library cataloguing in publication data

Donaldson, Morag L.
Children's explanations:
A psycholinguistic study.
1. Language acquisition
I. Title
401'.9   P118

Library of Congress cataloguing in publication data

Donaldson, Morag L.
Children's explanations.
Based on the author's thesis
(PhD – University of Edinburgh, 1983).
Bibliography.
Includes index.
1. Psycholinguistics – Techniques.
2. Children – Language.   3. Thought and thinking.
4. Association of ideas.   I. Title.
BF463.M4D65   1986   155.4'13   86–4209

ISBN 0 521 32006 2

Contents

Illustrations

Tables

Acknowledgements

This book is based on my PhD thesis, which was submitted to the University of Edinburgh in 1983. I am grateful to all the people who have helped me while I was carrying out the research, writing the thesis, and converting it into a book.

My greatest debt of gratitude is to my supervisor, Alison Elliot, for her skilful and sensitive supervision. She provided me with invaluable advice, support and encouragement, but without threatening my independence. Many of the ideas expressed in this book took shape during the numerous stimulating discussions we had together.

Other members of the Department of Psychology at Edinburgh University also contributed to my research in various ways. I am particularly grateful to Margaret Donaldson, Roger Barrow and Carol Macdonald for many informal and fruitful discussions. Tom Pitcairn gave me useful advice concerning the stimuli for Experiment 2. Janet Panther gave very generously of her time and talents in drawing the pictures for the experiments.

I am grateful to Paul Harris and Terry Myers, who were the examiners for my PhD thesis. The useful and encouraging comments which they made at the 'viva' provided the basis for some of the revisions I have made to convert the thesis into a book. I am also indebted to the publishers' referees for their constructive suggestions, and to Penny Carter of Cambridge University Press for her helpful advice.

My colleagues in the Psychology Department at Plymouth Polytechnic provided me with day-to-day encouragement while I was converting the thesis into a book. In particular, thanks are due to Michael Hyland for commenting on some of the revised sections.

My family have been a constant source of support. As usual my sister, Fiona, assisted me with various practical matters, such as acting out the sequences for Experiment 4.

I would like to thank Cynthia Dunn and Siobhan Breslin for their efficient typing of the original and revised manuscripts.

The research reported in this book was supported by a studentship from the Social Science Research Council. Lothian Region's Education Committee kindly allowed me access to several primary schools: Granton Primary,

Acknowledgements

Musselburgh Burgh Primary, Trinity Primary and Wardie Primary. I gratefully acknowledge the friendly cooperation of the staff at these schools, at the Edinburgh University Psychology Department Nursery, and at Stoke Damerel Primary in Plymouth.

Thanks are also due to the undergraduates who took part in the adult studies, and to the lecturers in the Departments of Psychology and Linguistics at Edinburgh University who helped in the recruitment of volunteers.

Finally, I would like to express my gratitude to all the children who participated in the experiments, and who helped to ensure that no two days were alike.

1   Introduction

1.1 The ability to explain

Why do we give explanations? There are two main possibilities. We may give an explanation to help someone else understand something; alternatively, we may give an explanation to demonstrate our own understanding. Similarly, when we ask for an explanation, we may be aiming to extend our own understanding; alternatively, we may be aiming to test someone else's understanding. Thus, explanation provides both a means of conveying knowledge and a means of assessing knowledge. For this reason, explanation is central to education. The ability to give explanations, the ability to understand explanations, and the ability to seek explanations are important assets for both the teacher and the pupil. This brings us to the question which will be the major focus of this book: how and when does the ability to explain develop? Despite the considerable educational relevance of this question, there is a dearth of research which addresses it directly.

Developmental psychologists have tended to treat children's explanations and justifications not as subjects of study in their own right but rather as a research tool. In other words, researchers have used explanations as a means of assessing abilities other than the ability to explain. For example, children's explanations have been employed as measures of their understanding of causality (Piaget, 1929, 1930; Berzonsky, 1971), their social sensitivity (Flavell *et al.*, 1968), their metacognitive ability (Piaget, 1976, 1978), and their metalinguistic ability (Gleitman, Gleitman and Shipley, 1972). An implicit assumption underlying all such studies is that the children already possess the linguistic and cognitive resources which are required to produce explanations, and therefore that failure to produce an adequate explanation is attributable to a deficit in the ability under investigation. In this book, I shall assess the validity of such an assumption by examining the development of the ability to explain. If children's explanations are to be used as a window to their minds, then it is important to determine whether the window is truly transparent.

In our daily lives, we are likely to have to give various types of explanation. (See section 1.4.) We may be asked to explain an event (*Why did the car break down?*), or an action (*Why did you shut the door?*), or a conclusion (*How did you know it was going to rain?*), or a procedure (*Can you tell me how to bake a cake?*). In assessing children's ability to explain, I shall focus on their ability to deal with explanations of events, actions and conclusions.

1.2 Cognitive and linguistic aspects of explanation

Explanation is one of the many areas where language and cognition interact in an interesting manner. Although explaining is essentially a verbal activity in that we cannot explain without using language, the ability to explain does presuppose a number of cognitive abilities. For instance, the speaker has to be able to distinguish between a cause and an effect, between a reason and a result, and between a piece of evidence and a conclusion. Also, the content of the explanation has to be appropriate to the type of phenomenon being explained, and this, in turn, presupposes that the speaker has some under- standing of the phenomenon. However, the speaker will not be able to give an explanation unless he also has adequate linguistic resources. In particular, it is important that he be able to use the causal connectives, *because* and *so*, appropriately, since they serve to make the links explicit and also to signal which clause refers to the cause and which to the effect.

The knowledge which a speaker has to have in order to use *because* and *so* correctly is closely related to the knowledge which he requires in order to produce adequate explanations. The cognitive abilities which have just been outlined are prerequisites of the ability to use the causal connectives appro- priately. In addition, the speaker requires some specifically linguistic know- ledge about how each connective is used and about the distinction between the two connectives. However, it will be argued (in sections 1.4 and 1.5) that an adequate linguistic analysis of the causal connectives has to take into account the way the connectives function in various types of explanation. Thus, the ability to explain and the ability to use the causal connectives are closely intertwined. It is therefore possible to approach the development of explanation by investigating the development of the comprehension and production of the causal connectives, and this is the strategy which will be adopted in this book.[1] However, it should be emphasised that the comprehen- sion and production of the connectives will be studied in relation to the way the connectives function in various types of explanation. In this respect, the present study differs from most previous studies of the development of the connectives. (See Chapter 2.) Previous studies have usually failed to take sufficient account of the relationships between the types of explanation and the use of the causal connectives, and this has resulted in a rather restricted and distorted picture of the child's knowledge of the connectives' meaning.

1.3 The content of explanations

Very many phenomena could serve as the topics of explanations. Therefore, an exhaustive investigation of the effect of content on the child's ability to explain could not be carried out. However, one way of making the task more tractable is to group the phenomena into a small number of general content categories. In this study, three such categories will be distinguished: physical, psychological and logical.[2] This taxonomy is based on the types of laws or rules which would have to be invoked to account for the relation which holds between the elements referred to in the explanation. Relations in the physical category would be accounted for in terms of laws of physical causality. Psychological relations draw on notions of psychological causality, such as motivation and the reasons for actions. Logical relations are based on logical or arbitrary rules. The following sentences illustrate the three categories:

(1.1) *The window broke because a ball hit it.* (Physical)
(1.2) *Mary hit John because he pulled her hair.* (Psychological)
(1.3) *Half nine is not four because four and four make eight.* (Logical)

These content categories are based on the three types of causal relation which Piaget (1926, 1928) distinguishes. However, the definitions of the categories have been modified slightly for a reason which will become apparent after some further distinctions have been introduced. (See section 1.4.2.)

In this book, I shall be concerned with two questions regarding the content of explanations:

(i) Does the content category affect the children's ability to explain and to deal with the causal connectives?
(ii) Can the children differentiate appropriately among the content categories?

Both questions will be addressed in the experimental chapters which follow.

1.4 The modes of explanation

1.4.1 *The four modes*

In giving an explanation, the speaker is attempting to provide an answer to a question (even though the question is not always made explicit). This question may be either a *Why?* question or a *How?* question. If it is a *Why?* question, then it may be interpreted either as being equivalent to a *What has happened to cause...?* question or as being equivalent to a *For what purpose...?* question. The *How?* questions can be sub-divided into *How do you know that...?* questions and *How do you DO...?* questions, where DO can be replaced by most dynamic verbs (e.g. *How do you bake a cake?*).

I shall propose that, corresponding to these four types of question, there are four different types of explanation which will be termed the 'modes of explanation': empirical, intentional, deductive and procedural. Each mode can be defined in terms of the speaker's aim in giving an explanation, and in terms of the way he views the phenomenon which he is explaining. Also, each mode has associated with it a characteristic set of linguistic structures. (See Table 1 in section 1.4.2.)

In giving an empirical explanation, the speaker's aim is to provide an answer to the *What has happened to cause...?* version of the *Why?* question. He views the phenomenon he is explaining as an event or state which requires an explanation in terms of a temporally prior event or state. While there may be a certain amount of temporal overlap between the two events/states, an empirical explanation cannot refer to an event/state which begins *after* the event/state being explained.

The speaker's aim in giving an intentional explanation is to answer the *For what purpose ...?* version of the *Why?* question. He views the phenomenon he is explaining as an action, as a goal-directed and purposive element of behaviour, which requires an explanation in terms of an aim or intention. Unlike empirical explanations, intentional explanations are 'forward-looking' in that they include a reference to an event or state which occurs, or is expected to occur, *after* the action which is being explained.

When the speaker gives a deductive explanation, his aim is to provide an answer to a *How do you know that...?* question. He views the phenomenon as an idea, a concept, a judgement, or a conclusion. It is a 'mental act' which requires an explanation or justification in terms of either another mental act, or a rule, or some observable evidence.

The speaker's aim in giving a procedural explanation is to answer a *How do you DO...?* question. His task is to outline the steps leading up to a particular goal in such a way that his description would tell the listener what he would have to do in order to achieve the goal. For example, many of the explanations given in cookery books or in instruction manuals would fall into the procedural category. Typically, the steps in the procedure are mentioned in chronological order, and information about temporal order is often more important than information about causality in this explanatory mode. Therefore, the links in a procedural explanation are more likely to be made explicit by means of temporal connectives (e.g. *now, first, then*) than by means of causal connectives. For this reason, very little consideration will be given to procedural explanations in this book.

1.4.2. *The relationship between content and mode*

There is a certain amount of confusion in the literature as to whether the physical/psychological/logical distinction applies to the type of phenomenon which is being explained or to the way in which it is explained. Piaget (1928) distinguishes three types of causal relation: empirical, psychological and logical. He defines empirical relations as cause–effect relations between two events. Psychological relations are defined as holding between two psychological actions, or between an action and an intention, or between a psychological state and its psychological 'cause'. A logical relation holds between two ideas or judgements, or between a judgement and its proof or logical antecedent. These definitions have some features in common with my definitions of the content categories and some features in common with my definitions of the modes of explanation. The situation is further complicated by the fact that Piaget sometimes uses 'empirical relations' to include psychological relations, whereas at other times he equates empirical relations with causal explanations which, in turn, he equates with mechanical or physical explanations. In fact, it is the latter distinction (*physical*/psychological/logical) which has come to figure more prominently in Piaget's theory and in subsequent research on the development of the causal connectives and of notions of causality. Similarly, the features of the definition of the logical relation which have assumed the greatest prominence in subsequent research are those which correspond to my logical content category rather than to my deductive mode. However, it is worthwhile preserving both aspects of Piaget's rather ambiguous taxonomy, and this is the motivation for the distinction which I have drawn between the content and the mode of an explanation.

The content categories are based on the types of relations which hold between the events/states/actions/mental acts referred to in the explanation. These relations may be expressed linguistically. Nevertheless, they hold independently of their expression in language. In contrast, the modes of explanation are based on the speaker's view of his task and on how this affects the type of relation which he expresses in his explanation.

However, the two taxonomies are not totally independent of one another. It is not the case that any content category can be combined with any mode. There is a complex relationship between the content categories and the modes. This relationship is summarised in Table 1. Explanations in the empirical mode may express either physical or psychological relations. In giving an intentional explanation, the speaker asserts that a psychological relation holds between an action (e.g. *John wound up the toy car*) and an intention (e.g. *he wanted it to go.*). At the same time, the speaker presupposes that there is also a causal relation between the action and the effect which the agent is aiming to achieve. This presupposed relation may be either physical or psychological,

Table 1. *Summary of the relationship between content and mode*

Mode	Content Asserted	Presupposed	Example
Empirical	Physical	—	The window broke because a ball hit it.
Empirical	Psychological	—	Mary hit John because he pulled her hair.
Intentional	Psychological	Physical	John wound up the toy car because he wanted it to go.
Intentional	Psychological	Psychological	John put a mouse in Mary's bed because he wanted to frighten her.
Deductive	Logical	Physical	(We can tell that) the window broke because there is glass on the ground.
Deductive	Logical	Psychological	(We can tell that) Mary is sad because she is crying.
Deductive	Logical	—	(We can tell that) half nine is not four because four and four make eight.

and it can be made explicit by means of a sentence in the empirical mode:

(1.4) *The toy car went because John wound it up.*
(1.5) *Mary got a fright because John put a mouse in her bed.*

Thus, the intentional mode can be seen as being parasitic on the empirical mode. Because of this relationship, explanations in the intentional mode sometimes involve more than one type of content. A similar position obtains regarding the deductive mode. In giving a deductive explanation, the speaker asserts that a logical relation holds. However, the speaker's deduction may draw on his knowledge of a physical relation, such as:

(1.6) *There is glass on the ground because the window broke,*

or on his knowledge of a psychological relation, such as:

(1.7) *Mary is crying because she is sad.*

In such cases, the deductive explanation is parasitic on the empirical mode, and the deductive explanation involves two types of content. On the other hand, a deductive explanation may be based on knowledge of logical rules or relations, as in:

(1.8) *(We can tell that) half nine is not four because four and four make eight.*

In such cases, the deductive explanation is not parasitic on the empirical mode.

1.5 Linguistic analysis of the causal connectives

It was claimed earlier (see section 1.4.1) that there are differences of linguistic structure between the modes, and the examples presented in Table 1 illustrate some of these differences. However, I shall leave a detailed consideration of the linguistic characteristics of each mode until later. (See sections 4.1.2, 5.1.2 and 6.1.2.) In this section, a more general linguistic analysis of the causal connectives will be presented. At times, this account may be biased towards the empirical mode, since most of the studies reviewed in Chapter 2 are based on the empirical mode and since it is important to understand the assumptions underlying these studies.

The causal connectives lie in an area of overlap between semantics, syntax and pragmatics. In order to explore the nature of the interaction among these three areas, I shall adopt the strategy of focussing on the semantic approach, and then assessing its limitations.

Lyons (1977) distinguishes three types of meaning relation: sense, denotation and reference. Sense relations hold between linguistic expressions, rather than between a linguistic expression and an entity in the world. One of the sense relations which Lyons identifies is the relation of converseness, and it could be argued that this relation holds between *because* and *so*. When the relation of converseness holds, it is possible to substitute one member of the converse pair for the other in a sentence and to transpose the relevant terms without altering the truth-conditions of the sentence. In other words, if *because* and *so* are members of a converse pair, then *X so Y* should be equivalent to *Y because X*.[3] The equivalence of pairs of sentences, such as the following, suggests that the relation of converseness does hold between *because* and *so*:

(1.9a) *A ball hit the window so the window broke.*
(1.9b) *The window broke because a ball hit the window.*

(1.10a) *John wanted to frighten Mary so he put a mouse in her bed.*
(1.10b) *John put a mouse in Mary's bed because he wanted to frighten her.*

(1.11a) *Four and four make eight so we can tell that half nine is not four.*
(1.11b) *We can tell that half nine is not four because four and four make eight.*

As for other converse pairs, the order of the elements is important in sentences containing *because* or *so*. When one member of a converse pair is substituted for the other without the remaining parts of the sentence being transposed, the new sentence expresses a proposition which is the converse of the proposition expressed by the original sentence. Therefore, there is a contrast in meaning between *X so Y* and *X because Y*. Similarly, there is a meaning contrast between sentences which differ with respect to the order of the clauses while the connective remains the same. Such a contrast holds between *X because Y* and *Y because X*, and between *X so Y* and *Y so X*. It is interesting to note that the relation of converseness holds only when the connective occurs in the sentence-medial position. When *because* occurs in sentence-initial position, it cannot be replaced by *so*:

(1.12a) *Because a ball hit the window, the window broke.*
(1.12b) **So the window broke, a ball hit the window.*

The contrast in meaning between *Because X, Y* and *X because Y* is equivalent to the meaning contrasts between the other pairs of sentences mentioned above.

The nature of these meaning contrasts is such that the two propositions expressed by the sentences in a contrasting pair cannot both be true of the same situation. However, in order to consider how one would decide which sentence expresses a true proposition, we must move beyond the notion of sense, and examine the meaning relations which hold between linguistic expressions and the world.

Lyons defines 'denotation' as the relationship which holds between a linguistic expression and the class of persons, things, places, properties, processes and activities external to the language system to which the expression correctly applies. The relation of denotation holds independently of particular occasions of utterance. In contrast, the relation of reference is an utterance-bound relation which holds of expressions in context. The notion of reference applies to the speaker's use of a linguistic expression to pick out an entity or group of entities.

The causal *connectives* have neither denotation nor reference. It simply does not make sense to ask what class of entities or properties *because* applies to. On the other hand, it does make sense to ask about the language–world relationship with respect to sentences containing the causal connectives, and to ask about the causal connectives' influence on that relationship. Lyons' notions of denotation and reference cannot readily be applied to sentences. In particular, he restricts the notion of reference to expressions which serve to identify entities. However, it seems worthwhile preserving the distinction between the class of properties etc. to which a linguistic expression correctly applies and the way in which the linguistic expression is used on a particular occasion. There seems to be no reason, in principle, why this distinction should not be applied to the relationship between sentences and the situations, events or sequences of events which they may be used to describe. In very general terms, the distinction corresponds to a distinction between semantics and pragmatics.

From a semantic point of view, the pertinent question is: which types of situations or sequences of events can sentences of the form *X so Y* or *Y because X* be applied to correctly? These sentences could be assigned a semantic representation of the form: CAUSE (X, Y), where CAUSE is a two-place predicate and X and Y are its arguments.[4] This captures the fact that the relation between X and Y is a causal one, and also that it is ordered. We can now say that the relation of converseness which holds between *because* and *so* is based on the fact that *because* signals that the following clause is a description of a cause, whereas *so* signals that the following clause is a description of an effect. The situations to which *X so Y* and *Y because X* are applicable are those situations which involve a causal relation between X and Y such that X is the cause and Y the effect. If X and Y are events, then X will be temporally prior to Y, since a cause begins before its effect. Thus, sentences containing *because* or *so* can convey information about temporal order.[5] However, this information is derived from the information which they convey about causal direction, and from the nature of causality.

In order to decide whether or not a particular sentence is being used to express a true proposition, it is necessary to move into the realm of pragmatics and to consider the way in which the sentence is being used in a particular context of utterance. The characteristics of the causal relation are dependent on the mode of explanation, and this has certain linguistic consequences. In particular, a linguistic expression may correspond to a true proposition if it is being used in the deductive mode and yet correspond to a false proposition if it is being used in the empirical mode. (See section 6.1.2.) An example of this would be:

(1.13) *Mary is sad because she is crying.*

In the light of this evidence, it is necessary to modify my earlier claim that the two propositions expressed by the sentences in a contrasting pair (e.g. *X because Y* and *Y because X*) cannot both be true. This claim holds only if both sentences are being used in the same mode.

The linguistic structure of the clauses X and Y varies according to the explanatory mode. In the intentional mode, X contains a linguistic form which indicates that it is an intention rather than an event that is being referred to (e.g. *wanted to, was going to, would, could*). In the deductive mode, Y sometimes contains a linguistic form which indicates that a conclusion is being expressed (e.g. *can tell that, know that, must*). Also, when one considers the intentional mode, it becomes necessary to distinguish two uses of *so*. In all the modes, *so* may be used in the sense of 'therefore', but in the intentional mode *so* may also be used in the sense of 'so that' or 'in order that'. These linguistic characteristics of the intentional and deductive modes will be explored in more detail at the beginning of the relevant chapters. (See sections 5.1.2 and 6.1.2.)

1.6 Assessing children's linguistic knowledge

As we shall see in Chapter 2, different methods yield rather different pictures of children's ability to use and understand the causal connectives. In particular, children show an ability to use the causal connectives appropriately in their spontaneous speech from about the age of 3, yet the evidence from comprehension experiments seems to indicate that they do not understand the causal connectives until the age of 7 or even later. Similar discrepancies have been observed in other areas of developmental psycholinguistics (Bloom, 1974; Chapman and Miller, 1975; Donaldson, 1978; Donaldson, 1980; Hoenigmann-Stovall, 1982). These discrepancies are enigmatic in that they run counter to the traditional assumption that comprehension will always be either in advance of or equal to production. Moreover, the ability to use a form appropriately presupposes some understanding of the form, yet this understanding is not evident in the results of the comprehension experiments.

How might such discrepancies be explained? There are two main types of possible explanation. It might be argued that a discrepancy in results between comprehension and production studies reflects a genuine difference between comprehension ability and production ability. In other words, comprehension ability and production ability may develop independently and so may sometimes be out of phase. Alternatively, it might be argued that the discrepancy in results is attributable to methodological factors since different types of method are typically used to assess comprehension as opposed to production. Let us now consider each of these explanations in more detail.

The proposal that there may be a genuine discrepancy between comprehension and production raises the issue of the relationship between these two processes. There are at least three possible views of the comprehension/production relationship.

The first possible view would involve adopting Chomsky's approach and arguing that both processes are guided by a single store of linguistic knowledge which is neutral with respect to the comprehension/production distinction. However, such an approach could not readily account for discrepancies between comprehension and production without invoking a much more detailed analysis of the processes than is usually offered in this approach.

A second possibility would be that there are two separate stores of linguistic knowledge: one guiding comprehension and one guiding production. These stores would be separate in the sense that information could not readily be exchanged between them. This would mean that a considerable amount of linguistic knowledge would be represented in duplicate, since it would be in both stores. It would also mean that, at a given point in development, the two stores might be out of phase. This type of model, in which the representations for comprehension are distinct from the representations for production, has several proponents (Campbell, Macdonald and Dockrell, 1982; Straight, 1982; Clark and Hecht, 1983; Margaret Donaldson, personal communication). Clark and Hecht use the model to account for cases in which comprehension is ahead of production, and they argue that the opposite discrepancy (production being ahead of comprehension) never occurs. The other proponents of the 'dual representation' model allow for the possibility of production sometimes being more advanced than comprehension. Essentially, they would argue that if the production store contains some linguistic knowledge which the comprehension store lacks, then production will be superior to comprehension in that particular area, since the comprehension process will not have access to information which is only in the production store. This type of argument does face a problem (although probably not an insurmountable one) in accounting for how knowledge in the production store could be acquired other than through comprehension.

A third possible approach would be to argue that the comprehension and production processes both have access to the same store of linguistic knowledge, but that the two processes differ with respect to the type of knowledge which they require. Thus, discrepancies in performance between comprehension and production would be attributed to the differential demands of the two processes rather than to the differential accessibility of a particular item of linguistic knowledge. These differential demands are related to differences between the task of being a speaker and the task of being a listener in a natural communication situation. Some of these differences work in favour of comprehension while others work in favour of production. For example, comprehension is usually supported by cues from the linguistic and non-linguistic context. Therefore, a listener can use various strategies which allow the message to be understood without complete comprehension of every word and of every aspect of the syntactic construction. On the other hand, one major advantage of being a speaker rather than a listener is that you usually have more choice or control over the content and form of the message. Consequently, you can select or avoid particular words and syntactic constructions and so keep within the bounds of your own competence. Arguments based on the differential demands of the speaker and listener roles have been put forward by Clark, Hutcheson and Van Buren (1974), by Chapman and Miller (1975) and by Hagtvet (1982).

Let us now turn to the second type of explanation of comprehension/ production discrepancies: that these discrepancies are attributable to methodological differences between comprehension and production studies. There is a certain amount of overlap between this position and the third view of the relationship between comprehension and production. Both are concerned with differential demands. However, the 'methodological' explanation deals with the differential demands imposed by comprehension and production studies, rather than with the differences between being a speaker and being a listener in a natural communication situation. The two types of differential demands coincide in some but not all cases.

Children's comprehension of linguistic forms is usually assessed by means of experimental rather than observational studies, because of the difficulty of controlling for contextual cues when dealing with comprehension in a natural setting. Thus, while comprehension of normal discourse may be assisted by contextual cues, this advantage does not usually carry over to comprehension studies. In contrast, children's production of linguistic forms is usually assessed by means of observational methods or experiments which are less constrained than those typically used to assess comprehension. Thus, the advantages of being a speaker, as outlined above, usually do carry over to production studies. In a production study, children normally have a considerable degree of choice about the content and form of their utterances. This may help to account for some comprehension/production discrepancies: if knowledge of a linguistic form or construction is initially restricted to particular contexts or to particular content areas, then this limitation in ability will be more likely to become apparent in a comprehension study than in a production study. Elicited production studies may provide a useful compromise in this respect, in that they enable the investigator to exercise more control over the content of the children's utterances than is possible in observational studies of production, but without introducing the other constraints commonly associated with comprehension experiments.

One of the major differences between comprehension and production studies concerns the balance of choice or control between the child and the investigator. In comprehension studies, most of the control typically rests with the investigator, whereas in production studies the balance of control tends to be with the child. As for the speaker/listener comparison, this difference in control applies to the content and the form of utterances, but there is also a third respect in which it is relevant to a comparison between comprehension and production studies. The design of a comprehension experiment usually reflects the investigator's assumptions about the nature of the knowledge which underlies linguistic comprehension. Very often, the comprehension experiment is designed to test for one particular aspect of the meaning of a word and 'irrelevant' cues are deliberately excluded to aid interpretation of the children's performance. Consequently, if the investigator's assumptions are not consistent with the type of knowledge which guides the children's comprehension and production of the word in normal discourse, then the children may fail in the comprehension experiment even though they have some knowledge of the word's meaning. In production studies, the children typically have much more control over the type of knowledge they use to achieve success. They do not necessarily have to use the particular type of knowledge which the investigator believes is relevant. Thus, there is an asymmetry between comprehension studies and production studies. The advantage of comprehension studies is that they can identify the *particular type* of knowledge which children possess about a word's meaning, but they are less useful as a means of establishing whether or not children have *some* knowledge of the word's meaning. On the other hand, the advantage of production studies is that they can establish whether or not children have some knowledge of the word's meaning, but they are less useful as a means of identifying the precise nature of the knowledge. This asymmetry may account for some of the comprehension/production discrepancies. It also implies that production studies should be carried out before comprehension studies, since it makes sense to establish whether or not some knowledge is present before trying to investigate the nature of the knowledge. This is the approach adopted in the present study.

Linguistic knowledge may be used not only to guide the comprehension and production processes, but also as a basis for making judgements about language. Some studies have attempted to assess children's linguistic knowledge by asking them to carry out metalinguistic tasks, such as judging the acceptability of sentences or the synonymy of pairs of sentences. Metalinguistic tasks require the children to reflect on and comment on language, rather than to use language to express a message or to obtain a message. While children's success in these tasks is dependent on their having linguistic knowledge of the relevant forms or constructions, failure does not necessarily imply that they lack such knowledge. For instance, it may be that, initially, children's linguistic knowledge is not at a sufficiently high level of awareness to be used as a basis for metalinguistic judgements. This proposal has received some support from recent research (e.g. from some of the studies reported in Sinclair, Jarvella and Levelt, 1978). Although the issue of metalinguistic awareness will not be investigated directly in this book, it is relevant to the assessment of some of the tasks which have been used to study children's knowledge of the causal connectives' meaning. (See section 2.1.2.)

One lesson to be learnt from the fact that different methods yield different results is that it is not appropriate to ask whether the child knows what a particular word means. We must rather ask: what type of knowledge (if any) does the child have about the meaning of the word, and how does this knowledge develop?

1.7 Hypotheses about the development of the causal connectives

A number of hypotheses about the development of the causal connectives can be derived from the arguments presented in sections 1.5 and 1.6.

One hypothesis would be that the development consists of an increase in the child's knowledge of the directional element of the causal connectives' meaning. In other words, the child acquires the knowledge that *Y because X*, *X so Y* and *Because X, Y* all express the proposition CAUSE (X, Y) and not the proposition CAUSE (Y, X). All the previous studies of the development of the causal connectives have aimed to test this hypothesis. If a child treats *Y because X* (or any of the equivalent constructions) as if it corresponded to CAUSE (Y, X), then he is said to have produced an inversion of the cause–effect relation. These inversions are assumed to be indicative of a lack of knowledge of the directional element of the causal connectives' meaning. Therefore, the hypothesis predicts that the frequency of inversions will decrease as children grow older. As we shall see in Chapter 2, previous studies have yielded conflicting results regarding this hypothesis. Children's spontaneous production of the causal connectives indicates that inversions are very rare even among 2- to 3-year-olds and therefore that there is very little development in children's knowledge of the directional element. On the other hand, the results of most of the comprehension experiments suggest that such knowledge does develop up to the age of about 7 or 8.

A second hypothesis would be that the particular type of knowledge assessed by the comprehension experiments differs from that which guides the children's comprehension and production of the causal connectives in normal discourse. Thus, rather than involving the acquisition of the directional element, development would involve a change in the nature of the child's knowledge of the directional element. The primary function of the causal connectives, *because* and *so*, is to convey information about the direction of a causal relation. These connectives can also convey information about temporal order, but this information is derived from the information which they convey about causal direction via the hearer's knowledge of the nature of causality. Therefore, indicating the temporal order of events is a secondary function of the causal connectives.[6] Most of the previous comprehension experiments have employed tasks which require the children to base their responses on the causal connectives' secondary function of indicating temporal order. In order to succeed in such tasks, the children would have to know that *because* introduces the event which happened first whereas *so* introduces the event which happened second. However, it may be that children's knowledge of the directional element of the causal connectives' meaning is based initially on their primary function of indicating causal direction. In other words, the children may know that *because* introduces a cause whereas *so* introduces an effect, without knowing that *because* introduces the first event whereas *so* introduces the second event.[7] This will be referred to as the 'causal direction hypothesis'. The young child's lack of knowledge about the connectives' secondary function of indicating temporal order would tend to go unnoticed in production studies, but would become apparent in comprehension experiments involving temporal order tasks. The causal direction hypothesis would predict that if a comprehension experiment were carried out which allowed children to base their responses on knowledge of the causal connectives' primary function of indicating causal direction, then performance would be better than in a comprehension experiment requiring knowledge of their secondary function of indicating temporal order. The experiment reported in Chapter 4 was designed to test this prediction.

A third hypothesis would be that the child's knowledge of the causal connectives' meaning is initially restricted to one of the content categories. (See section 1.3.) The development of the connectives would then involve the extension and elaboration of this knowledge to include other content areas. In particular, Piaget (1926) proposed that children understand psychological relations before physical or logical relations. This hypothesis would predict either that young children will invert the cause–effect relation more frequently for non-psychological relations than for psychological relations, or that young children will tend to 'convert' non-psychological relations into psychological relations (or both). Both of these predictions are tested by the elicited production studies reported in Chapter 3. The first prediction is also tested in Experiments 4 to 7.

A fourth hypothesis would be that the child's knowledge of the causal connectives is initially restricted in terms of the mode of explanation. For instance, since the empirical mode is more basic than the intentional and deductive modes (see section 1.4), the child might begin by comprehending and producing the connectives appropriately only in the empirical mode. Therefore, the development of the connectives would involve the child's knowledge being extended and modified to take account of the other modes. Such a development might be either cognitive or linguistic (or both), since the modes differ both in terms of the cognitive demands and in terms of the linguistic demands which they impose on the child. This hypothesis is tested by the experiments reported in Chapters 4 (empirical), 5 (intentional) and 6 (deductive).

1.8 Outline of the book

In Chapter 2, previous research on the development of the causal connectives and on the development of causality is reviewed. It becomes apparent that there is a discrepancy between the results of the comprehension experiments and the results of naturalistic studies of children's production of the causal connectives. However, there is a dearth of systematic studies of children's production of the causal connectives, especially during the preschool period.

Chapter 3 reports three elicited production studies which were carried out with 3- to 5-year-olds in order to provide data on young children's production of the causal connectives in an experimental setting. The results are consistent with the findings of previous production studies, and therefore the need for an explanation of the comprehension/production discrepancy is confirmed.

In Chapter 4, the causal direction hypothesis is put forward as a possible explanation of the discrepancy, and an experiment is reported which tests and supports this hypothesis. Like most previous experiments, this experiment is based on the empirical mode.

The tendency to concentrate on studying empirical explanations is likely to result in a restricted picture (and perhaps even a distorted picture) of children's knowledge of the causal connectives' meaning. Therefore, the remaining experimental chapters seek to extend this picture by investigating children's knowledge of the causal connectives in relation to the intentional mode (Chapter 5) and the deductive mode (Chapter 6).

2 The development of the causal connectives and of causality: some previous studies

2.1 Children's comprehension and production of causal connectives

2.1.1 *Piaget's theory and research*

Piaget's work yields two main hypotheses regarding children's comprehension and production of the causal connectives:

(a) Children younger than about 7 or 8 years will tend to invert the cause–effect relation when they are producing and comprehending causal sentences.
(b) Children younger than about 7 or 8 years will fail to differentiate among physical, psychological and logical relations, and will tend to over-generalise the psychological relations. They will understand psychological relations first, then physical relations, and finally logical relations.

Piaget's own research provides some support for these hypotheses.

Piaget (1926) reports an experiment in which 6- to 8-year-olds were told a story or given an explanation of a mechanical object by the experimenter, and were then asked to reproduce the story or explanation to another child of the same age. Although Piaget does not give any detailed numerical results, he states that the children rarely expressed causal relations explicitly, but rather tended to juxtapose statements. Moreover, Piaget claims that even when the children did link two statements with (the French equivalent of) *because*, they did not intend to express a directional causal relation:

because does not yet denote an unambiguous relation of cause and effect, but something much vaguer and more undifferentiated, which may be called the 'relation of juxtaposition', and which can best be rendered by the word *and*...When the child replaces *and* by *because*, he means to denote, sometimes the relation of cause and effect, sometimes the relation of effect and cause. (p. 116)

In support of this claim, Piaget quotes some examples from his data of uses of *because* which involved inversions of the cause–effect relation, but he does not report the frequency of such inversions. Piaget does not make a specific prediction about the relative frequencies of correct and inverted uses of *because.* On the other hand, he gives us no reason to suppose that the child will systematically favour one of the two causal directions, and so he can be interpreted as implying that correct and inverted uses of *because* will be equally likely.

Later, Piaget (1928) reports a more systematic study of children's understanding of *because*, in which a written sentence completion task was administered to 7- to 9-year-olds. The children were asked to write completions for the following sentence fragments:

(2.1) *I shan't go to school tomorrow, because...*
(2.2) *That man fell off his bicycle, because...*
(2.3) *Paul says he saw a little cat swallowing a big dog. His friend says that is impossible (or silly) because...*
(2.4) *Half nine is not four because...*

Piaget predicted that the sentences involving empirical *because* ((2.1) and (2.2)) would be easier than those involving logical *because* ((2.3) and (2.4)), and the results support this prediction. Piaget regards a given age group as having succeeded on an item when 75% of the children pass. On the basis of this criterion, success is achieved on (2.1) at 7 years, on (2.2) at 8 years, and on (2.3) at 9 years. None of the age groups tested succeeded in (2.4). Piaget concludes that correct use of empirical *because* begins between the ages of 7 and 8, and that logical *because* develops later. However, he pays very little attention to the variations in results which occur between items of the same type. In particular, he fails to comment on the significance of the fact that 85% of the 7-year-olds passed the first item – a fact which suggests that even younger children might have been capable of passing this item (if it had been presented in an oral rather than a written form).[1] Thus, Piaget's research does not establish the lower limit of children's ability to handle *because*.

2.1.2 *Metalinguistic tasks*

(a) *Acceptability tasks*
These tasks are based on the assumption that children's knowledge of the causal connectives' meaning will be reflected in their ability to judge the acceptability of sentences containing causal connectives. Some studies (Epstein, 1972; Corrigan, 1975; Emerson, 1979) have used tasks which require children to make judgements about the absolute acceptability of sentences. For each item in these tasks, the children were presented with a single sentence which they were required to judge as acceptable or unacceptable. The terms which were used to convey the acceptable/unacceptable distinction to the children vary from study to study. Corrigan asked her subjects to say whether the sentence was 'yes or no, right or wrong', while

Emerson used the terms 'sensible' and 'silly'. Epstein's subjects were asked to say whether they thought the sentence had been produced by a 'silly' lady or by an 'okay' lady. The studies also vary with respect to the age of the subjects and the types of sentences used. Corrigan tested 3- to 7-year-olds, while Epstein and Emerson both tested 6- to 11-year-olds. Corrigan and Emerson used only sentence-medial *because* sentences. Epstein used four types of sentence: *so* sentences, *and* sentences, and both types of *because* sentence (sentence-medial and sentence-initial). In all the studies, half of the sentences were acceptable and half were unacceptable. In Corrigan's study, both types of item were sub-divided into physical, affective and logical items. (These categories are similar to Piaget's physical, psychological and logical categories.)

Corrigan's results provide some support for Piaget's hypothesis about the order of emergence of the relations expressed by *because*, in that performance was best on the affective items and worst on the logical items. Corrigan also found that performance was much better for acceptable items than for unacceptable items. In discussing the results, Corrigan stresses the more negative aspects, such as the fact that the younger children performed badly on the logical items, and she suggests that the attainment of concrete operations may be a prerequisite for understanding the logical use of *because*. However, it was only on the unacceptable items that the younger children performed really badly. For example, 70% of the 4-year-olds passed on the acceptable logical items, whereas none of them passed on the unacceptable logical items.

Epstein and Emerson also found that performance was much better on acceptable items than on unacceptable items. They both argue that children should not be credited with knowledge of the connectives' meaning until they have succeeded in both types of item. On this basis, the authors conclude that full knowledge of the connectives' meaning is not acquired until between the ages of about 10 and 12 years.

There are, however, a number of problems associated with the method employed by Corrigan, Epstein and Emerson. First, there is the problem of interpreting the discrepancy between performance on acceptable items and performance on unacceptable items. One plausible explanation of this discrepancy would be that the children have a tendency to acquiesce and that this may mask their knowledge. This could result in false positives on acceptable items and false negatives on unacceptable items. Therefore, by requiring correct performance on unacceptable as well as acceptable items, Epstein and Emerson may under-estimate the children's knowledge of the connectives' meaning.

A second, and related, problem is that the request for a judgement about the absolute acceptability of a sentence implies that there is a clear-cut distinction between acceptable and unacceptable sentences. We have already seen that this is not a valid assumption, since a sentence may be interpreted in a variety of ways depending on the context in which it is used. When a sentence is presented out of context (as in these studies), the subjects are likely to construct a context on which to base their interpretation of the sentence. If the subjects are accustomed to making use of the assumption that what a speaker says will make sense,[2] then it is reasonable to suppose that they will attempt to construct a context which will render the sentence acceptable. Therefore, the indeterminacy will tend to be resolved as an 'acceptable' rather than as an 'unacceptable' judgement. Emerson actually admits that the unacceptable sentences may be simply less plausible than the acceptable sentences, rather than being totally unacceptable. She then says that children's understanding of *because* can be assessed by looking at their ability to judge an inverted sentence as less acceptable than the corresponding correct-order sentence. However, this is not what she asked her subjects to do. They had to make absolute rather than relative judgements. Indeed, each subject received either the inverted version or the correct version of a given sentence, but not both.

A third problem is that children may be basing their judgements on the semantic content of the two clauses rather than on the way the connective is being used. In other words, they will judge a sentence as acceptable if each of its clauses describes an event or state which is compatible with their view of the world. Since the connectives themselves have neither denotation nor reference, it would not be surprising if the children were to focus on the parts of the sentence which do have denotation or reference, when they are being asked a question about the match between language and the world. This problem is likely to have been particularly acute in Emerson's study, since she trained her subjects using a 'silly' item which was silly because of the relations between the content words within a single clause: *The dog drove the car*. This may have encouraged the children to focus on the semantic content of the clauses linked by the connective, rather than on the relationship between the connective and the order of the clauses. In addition to asking the children to judge the acceptability of the sentences, Emerson asked them to change the sentences which they judged 'silly' into 'sensible' sentences and vice versa. She found that, particularly among the younger subjects, the strategies used for converting 'silly' into 'sensible' sentences involved changing the content of one of the clauses. This suggests that the original judgements were based on the content of the clauses, rather than on the relation between the clauses. Emerson interprets this as evidence that young children do not know that *because* specifies the direction of the causal relation. She argues that the children focus on the semantic content of the clauses because of their lack of knowledge about *because*. However, an alternative interpretation would be that the children's apparent lack of knowledge of the directionality of *because* is due to their tendency to focus on the semantic content of the clauses, and that this tendency is in fact encouraged by Emerson's training procedure.

The problems associated with asking children to make judgements about the absolute acceptability of sentences can be avoided (or at least reduced) by asking children to make judgements about the relative acceptability of two or more sentences. This approach has been adopted in a number of studies (Katz and Brent, 1968; Kuhn and Phelps, 1976; Flores d'Arcais, 1978b). These studies differ from one another in several respects.

Katz and Brent were interested in studying various aspects of children's understanding of complex sentences, and their study included only one item which is relevant to the question of whether children understand the directionality of the causal connectives. For this item, the experimenter read out a correct *and* sentence and an inverted *because* sentence, and asked the child to choose the sentence which 'seemed better'. The two sentences were identical except for the connective. Katz and Brent found that, in all the age groups (6- to 7-year-olds, 11- to 12-year-olds, and adults), there was a strong preference for the non-inverted sentence. Even in the youngest group, 82% of the subjects chose the non-inverted sentence. Katz and Brent interpret this as evidence that 6- to 7-year-olds have a less ambiguous understanding of the meaning of *because* than Piaget would claim. However, Katz and Brent's method can be criticised on the grounds that the subjects might have chosen the non-inverted *and* sentence because they were more familiar with *and* than with *because*, rather than because they preferred non-inverted sentences to inverted sentences.

Kuhn and Phelps avoided this problem by using pairs of sentences which differed with respect to the order of the two clauses rather than with respect to the choice of connective. Half of the sentence-pairs consisted of *because*-initial sentences and half consisted of *because*-medial sentences. The child was presented with a picture of an event and with two written sentences. The experimenter read out the sentences and asked the child to choose the sentence which 'goes best with the picture'. Kuhn and Phelps tested a group of 5- to 8-year-olds. They found that most of the youngest group (mean = 5; 9) were responding randomly, whereas 67% of the middle group (mean = 6; 9) and 87% of the oldest group (mean = 7; 10) succeeded in the task (according to a criterion of 13/16 items correct). Kuhn and Phelps conclude that their results support Piaget's hypothesis, in that the youngest children did not seem to understand that *because* expresses a unidirectional relation between cause and effect.

Flores d'Arcais used a technique similar to Kuhn and Phelps' to study Dutch and Italian children's knowledge of the causal connectives. The main difference between the studies is that Flores d'Arcais asked his subjects to choose one sentence from a set of three sentences, whereas Kuhn and Phelps used pairs of sentences. Flores d'Arcais' results are broadly compatible with those of Kuhn and Phelps. Although he found that performance improved throughout the 7 to 12 age range, even the youngest subjects seemed to be responding at an above-chance level.

The results of the studies which call for judgements of relative acceptability suggest that children understand the directional element of *because* from the age of about 7 or 8. On the other hand, the results of Epstein's and Emerson's studies, which call for judgements of absolute acceptability, suggest that children do not understand the directional element of *because* until between the ages of 10 and 12. Epstein argues that the fact that children judge one sentence to be 'better' than another does not necessarily mean that they would not consider both sentences to be acceptable. However, the ability to make a systematically correct distinction between sentences which differ only in clause-order does imply an understanding of the directional element of the connectives' meaning. Moreover, it is probably much more reasonable to ask for relative judgements than to ask for absolute judgements, since a request for a relative judgement does not imply that there is a clear-cut distinction between acceptable and unacceptable sentences. In this connection, it is interesting to note that, in Epstein's and Emerson's tasks, not even the oldest children were giving responses which were 100% correct. Epstein comments that the children accepted a wider range of sentences than adults would, but she does not actually provide any adult data to support this claim. It may be that adults are also reluctant to draw a sharp dividing line between acceptable and unacceptable uses of the causal connectives. (See sections 6.4.1, 6.7.1 and 6.8.)

(b) Synonymy tasks
These tasks involve asking the child to judge whether or not two sentences (which differ with respect to the causal connective used or with respect to the position of the causal connective) are synonymous. Flores d'Arcais (1978b) presented 7- to 10-year-old Italian children and 7- to 12-year-old Dutch children with pairs of sentences which differed only in the connective used. For each sentence-pair, one sentence was acceptable and the other was unacceptable, so the two sentences were always non-synonymous.[3] First, the child was presented with the acceptable sentence. Then she was presented with the unacceptable sentence and was asked whether she could use it to tell another child about the event described in the first sentence. Flores d'Arcais found that only about 50% of the 7-year-olds' responses consisted of judgements that the two sentences were non-equivalent in meaning. Performance on the task improved considerably between the ages of 7 and 10 years. However, some of the problems which were encountered in relation

to the acceptability tasks which called for absolute judgements also arise in relation to this synonymy task. First, the testing procedure is likely to have directed the children's attention towards the content of the clauses, rather than towards the connectives, since the children were asked whether the two sentences could both be used to tell a friend about a particular *event*. If the children were basing their responses on the content of the clauses, then they would judge the sentences to be equivalent, since the content of the clauses was the same for both sentences. Second, a general tendency to acquiesce may also have encouraged the children to judge the sentences to be equivalent.

In Emerson and Gekoski's (1980) synonymy task, half of the sentence pairs were synonymous and half were non-synonymous. Within the synonymous category, half of the items consisted of an *X because Y* sentence and a *Because Y, X* sentence, and half consisted of an *X if Y* sentence and an *If Y, X* sentence. Within the non-synonymous category, half of the items consisted of an *X because Y* sentence and an *X then Y* sentence, and half consisted of an *X if Y* sentence and an *X so Y* sentence. For each item, the child was asked to select a picture sequence to match one of the sentences, and then this picture-selection task was repeated for the other sentence in the pair. Finally, the child was asked: 'Do these sentences mean the same thing?' Emerson and Gekoski found that performance was better on the synonymous items than on the non-synonymous items. This might be attributable to a tendency to acquiesce. The youngest subjects (mean = 6; 10) performed at a random level, and there was a significant improvement in performance between the middle age group (mean = 8; 0) and the oldest age group (mean = 9; 11). However, even the oldest group was not performing at ceiling level.

The results of the synonymy tasks suggest that the ability to make judgements about the synonymy of pairs of causal sentences develops relatively late. However, it is likely that this is one of the final stages in the development of children's knowledge of the causal connectives. The linguistic and cognitive demands involved in comparing two complex sentences are probably much greater than those involved in the comprehension and production of individual causal sentences in normal discourse.

2.1.3 *Memory tasks*

These tasks are based on the assumption that the errors which a child makes in imitating, recognising, or recalling causal sentences can provide information about the child's knowledge of the causal connectives.

Emerson and Gekoski (1980) used an imitation task in which subjects were asked to repeat *because* sentences immediately after the experimenter had read each sentence. Errors were more frequent in the youngest group (mean = 6; 10) than in the older groups, but even the youngest group performed at an above-chance level. Most of the errors made by the youngest group involved either omitting the connective or substituting one connective for another. Emerson and Gekoski interpret this as evidence that the youngest children were not always attending to the specific connective used. However, these omission and substitution errors account for only 13% of the youngest group's responses.

Emerson and Gekoski also used a recognition task in which children were presented with a target sentence, and were then required to judge whether or not each sentence in a larger set of sentences was exactly the same as the target. The rationale behind this task was that if the children had understood the meaning of the original sentence, they would tend to show false recognitions of sentences which preserved this meaning. For example, if the original sentence was of the form *Y because X*, then the children would be expected to show false recognitions of a sentence of the form *Because X, Y* which had the same content. The results indicated that the youngest children (the 6- to 7-year-olds) were tending to judge any sentence which contained the same two clauses as the target sentence as 'same', irrespective of the connective and of the clause order. For instance, a sentence with the form *Y then X* would be judged to be the same as the target sentence, *Y because X*. In contrast, the older children (especially the 10-year-olds) tended to restrict their judgements of 'same' to those sentences which preserved the original meaning. Emerson and Gekoski argue that the youngest children's poor performance was due to a failure to understand that the connective indicates a specific relation, and not to memory limitations. Their reason for making this claim is that the youngest children's performance was much better on control sentences which differed from the target sentence both with respect to the content of the subordinate clause and with respect to either the connective used or the clause order. In other words, the children were less likely to judge *Y then Z* as being the same as *Y because X* than they were to judge *Y then X* as being the same as *Y because X*. However, Emerson and Gekoski's control sentences merely serve as a check that the children are capable of remembering the subordinate clause. The fact that the youngest children can remember the content of the subordinate clause does not necessarily mean that their poor performance on the other sentences cannot be attributed to memory limitations. It is presumably easier to recognise gross differences between sentences, such as those produced by changing whole clauses, than to recognise the more subtle differences which are produced by changing a connective or the order of the clauses.

Epstein (1972) asked her subjects to recall each sentence after they had judged its acceptability. She found that performance was particularly poor for *so* sentences because the children showed a strong tendency to replace *so* with *because*. Epstein argues that since these substitutions did not consistently result in the production of acceptable sentences, they simply represent substitutions of preferred forms rather than attempts to recode the sentence's underlying meaning. Similarly, in discussing this study, Johnson and Chapman (1980) conclude that the recall task is not a reliable guide to the child's understanding of the meaning of the sentence. However, the fact that Epstein's subjects were being exposed to a mixture of acceptable and unacceptable sentences may have interfered with their interpretation of the sentences and with their ability to recode the sentence's meaning.

Flores d'Arcais (1978a) used a recall task involving only acceptable sentences. Sets of five sentences were presented to 6- to 9-year-old Italian children, and recall of each sentence was prompted by referring to a word in the sentence (e.g. 'Now repeat the sentence about the dog.'). The youngest children tended to recall subordinate constructions (which contained the equivalents of *because* and *in order to*) as coordinate constructions (which contained the equivalent of *and*). However, the children usually reproduced both the *B because A* sentences and the *A in order to B* sentences as *A and B*, rather than as *B and A*. This implies that they had some understanding of the directional relation between A and B, but this understanding might have been based either on knowledge of the connectives' meaning or on knowledge about the most probable relation between the two events. It is not possible to decide between these two alternatives, since Flores d'Arcais does not give details of the content of the stimulus sentences.

Both in the case of recognition tasks and in the case of recall tasks, positive results provide more conclusive evidence about the child's knowledge of the causal connectives' meaning than negative results do, since poor performance can usually be attributed either to a lack of knowledge of the connectives or to a memory deficit. For instance, the fact that the youngest children in Flores d'Arcais' recall task tended to recall *because* and *in order to* as *and* does not necessarily mean that they thought these connectives all had the same meaning. The task of remembering five sentences is likely to have imposed severe demands on the children's memories and this may have led them to make errors which do not reflect their actual knowledge of the connectives' meaning. On the other hand, children's performance on a memory task can sometimes provide evidence that they do understand the connectives' meaning, as when the older subjects in Emerson and Gekoski's recognition task produced false recognitions of sentences with the same meaning as the target sentence while rejecting those sentences which differed from the target sentence in meaning.

2.1.4 *Comprehension experiments*

(*a*) *Temporal order tasks*

As was pointed out in section 1.5, *because* and *so* can convey information about temporal order as well as about causal direction. A number of studies have investigated children's knowledge of the directional element of the meaning of *because* and *so* by testing their knowledge of the temporal order function of these connectives. In order words, these studies have required children to show that they know that the clause which immediately follows *because* refers to the event which happened first, whereas the clause which immediately follows *so* refers to the event which happened second.

If a child succeeds on a temporal order task, then we can conclude that she does understand the temporal order function of the causal connectives and therefore that she knows that their meaning includes a directional element. On the other hand, failure in a temporal order task is open to several alternative interpretations.

One possibility would be that the child lacks any knowledge of the directional element, and that for her *because* and *so* denote unordered, undifferentiated relations. The child may know that these connectives have something to do with causality, but she does not know that they are used to signal the direction of the relation. This is the Piagetian interpretation of the way young children understand the causal connectives.

A second possible interpretation would be that the child assumes that the order-of-mention corresponds to the order-of-occurrence of the events. This would lead her to treat both *because* and *so* as if they meant 'and then'. Therefore, in a temporal order task, she would pass the *so* items but fail the *because* items (when *because* occurred in sentence-medial position), since the order-of-mention corresponds to the order-of-occurrence for *so* sentences but not for *because* sentences. This interpretation is more compatible with Werner and Kaplan's theoretical approach than with Piaget's. Werner and Kaplan (1963) argue that the order expressed in early linguistic expressions corresponds to the order in which children perceive the events which they are describing. Similarly, Clark (1971) proposes that young children may find *X before Y* sentences easier to understand then *Y after X* sentences because the order-of-mention coincides with the order-of-occurrence for the *before* sentences but not for the *after* sentences. Some authors (Corrigan, 1975; Bebout, Segalowitz and White, 1980) have suggested that young children's understanding of the causal connectives is based on the assumption that the events are mentioned in chronological order. On the other hand, other authors (e.g. Emerson, 1979; Johnson and Chapman, 1980) have argued that the order-of-mention strategy is task specific, and that the children do not actually regard *because* as being equivalent to *and then*, but simply lack the knowledge that *because* signals the direction of the relation.

Most researchers in this area have adopted one of these two interpretations of the child's failure on a temporal order task. However, a third interpretation is also possible. The child may know that the meaning of *because* and *so* contains a directional element, but her knowledge of this directional element may be based on the causal connectives' function of signalling causal direction rather than on their function of signalling temporal order. This is the interpretation which will be defended in this book.

Keeping these three alternative interpretations in mind, let us now consider the findings of some comprehension experiments which have employed temporal order tasks. Sullivan (1972) presented 4- to 10-year-olds with a causal sentence and two pictures depicting the two elements mentioned in the sentence. She then asked the children to 'point to the picture that comes first'. Sullivan failed to find any clear trends in her results. However, it is worthwhile considering her study in some detail, since it serves to highlight some of the methodological problems which are likely to be encountered when a temporal order task is used to investigate children's knowledge of the causal connectives. One of the problems with Sullivan's study is that the instruction which she gave to her subjects ('point to the picture that comes first') is highly ambiguous. Sullivan's intention was to ask the subjects to identify the picture depicting the event which happened first. However, it would be just as reasonable to interpret 'the picture that comes first' as referring to the picture depicting the event which was mentioned first, or as referring to the picture which occupied the higher of the two positions on the table. A further problem arises from the fact that Sullivan presented unacceptable sentences as well as acceptable sentences. For an unacceptable sentence, such as *Because the boy broke his leg, he fell off his bicycle*, it is not clear whether the subjects are expected to identify the event which happened first by using the syntactic cues (which suggest that the boy broke his leg first) or by using their knowledge of the plausibility of the two alternative sequences (which would probably suggest that the boy fell off his bicycle first). A third problem with Sullivan's study is concerned with the fact that some of the sentences expressed an arbitrary relationship such as:

(2.5) *Because the boy is wearing a blue sweater, he is carrying some blocks.*

In such cases, it makes very little sense to ask which picture comes first. Most of the other temporal order tasks have avoided this problem by using only those items which refer to events that can readily be arranged in a temporal sequence. However, this constitutes a restriction of the scope of temporal order tasks, since the causal connectives are used to express relations not only between such events, but also between states, ideas and judgements which cannot meaningfully be arranged in a temporal sequence.

Epstein (1972) used a temporal sequencing task in which 6- to 11-year-olds were presented with a causal sentence and two pictures depicting the events mentioned in the sentence, and were asked two questions: 'What happened first?' and 'Then what happened?' Unlike the instruction used by Sullivan, these questions refer unambiguously to the order of occurrence of the events. However, like Sullivan, Epstein used both acceptable and unacceptable sentences, so for unacceptable sentences there were two possible responses: one based on the syntactic cues, and the other based on semantic plausibility. Epstein was aware of this ambiguity, so, at the beginning of the test, she trained the children to base their responses on semantic plausibility. For example, Epstein would teach the children that if the sentence was:

(2.6) *He got a cookie because he was happy*,

then the correct response to 'What happened first?' would be 'He got a cookie.' The results indicated that the tendency to base responses on semantic plausibility decreased with age, while the tendency to base responses on syntactic cues increased with age. Epstein interprets the younger children's failure to attend to the syntactic structure as evidence that they do not yet understand the order relations involved in the linguistic expression of causality. This is a curious conclusion in view of the fact that the training procedure actually encouraged the children to ignore the syntactic cues where these conflicted with semantic plausibility.

Epstein's task involved four types of sentence structure:

X and Y, X so Y, Y because X and *Because X, Y*.

Performance was significantly worse for the *Y because X* sentences than for any of the other types of sentence, and Epstein attributes this to the fact that the *Y because X* sentences are the only sentences for which the order-of-mention does not coincide with the order-of-occurrence of the events.

Emerson (1979) used two temporal order tasks: the picture-sequence task (PST) and the first/last task (FLT). In the PST, the child was presented with a causal sentence and two static picture-strips, each depicting both of the events referred to by the sentence. The two picture-strips in a given pair differed only with respect to the order in which the events were depicted. The child's task was to choose the picture-strip which 'goes with the sentence'. In the FLT, the child was presented with a causal sentence and two pictures, each of which depicted one of the events mentioned in the sentence. The child was asked to 'put the pictures in order to show what happened first and what happened last'. Both tasks were presented to a group of 6- to 11-year-olds, and the same sentences were used for both tasks. All the sentences were acceptable, and they all contained *because*. Half of the sentences were of the form *Y because X*, and half were of the form *Because X, Y*. Within each of these types, half of the sentences were non-reversible and half were reversible. For non-reversible sentences, one ordering of the events is plausible and the other ordering is implausible, whereas, for reversible sentences, both event-orders are plausible. Therefore, for non-reversible sentences, the semantic plausibility can act as a cue to the event-order, whereas, for reversible sentences, the connective used and the position of the connective are the only cues to the event-order. Emerson argues that the only conclusive evidence that the child fully understands *because* is successful performance on reversible *Y because X* items, since these are the only items for which it is not possible to respond correctly by relying either on semantic plausibility cues or on an order-of-mention strategy. On this basis, Emerson concludes that reliable responding on the PST occurred for the two older age groups (mean ages = 8; 2 and 10; 2) but not for the youngest group (mean = 6; 2). On the FLT, not even the oldest group achieved reliable responding.

The results of both the PST and the FLT provided some evidence in support of the hypothesis that the children were using an order-of-mention strategy, in that performance was better for *Because X, Y* items than for *Y because X* items. However, this effect was stronger for the FLT than for the PST, and Emerson interprets this as evidence that the order-of-mention strategy is, to a certain extent, task dependent. For this reason, Emerson argues that it is risky to assess comprehension on the basis of a single task. Similarly, she argues that studies which assess comprehension solely on the basis of performance on non-reversible sentences are likely to over-estimate the child's knowledge of the meaning of *because*, since they allow the child to make use of semantic plausibility cues. Although Emerson is aware that allowing children to make use of certain cues or strategies can result in their ability being over-estimated, she does not seem to be aware of the converse argument. Using a task which requires children to make use of knowledge which differs from the knowledge which guides their comprehension and production of *because* in normal discourse may result in their ability being under-estimated. In particular, Emerson uses children's failure on tasks requiring knowledge of the causal connectives' function of indicating temporal order as evidence that they have no knowledge of the directionality of the causal connectives.

Another type of task which requires children to base their responses on knowledge about the temporal order of events is the enactment task. Bebout, Segalowitz and White (1980) asked 5- to 10-year-olds to act out causal sentences using objects. The sentences were all reversible, and the only verb used was *move* (e.g. *The pencil moved so the car moved*). Three types of sentence construction were used: *X so Y*, *Y because X* and *Because X, Y*. Performance on the *Y because X* items was above chance-level only for the 9- to 10-year-olds, whereas performance on the other items was almost perfect even for the youngest subjects. Thus, the results suggest that the younger children may have been using an order-of-mention strategy.

Similar results were obtained by Flores d'Arcais (1978a) when he used an enactment task with 3- to 9-year-old Italian and Dutch children. Again, the younger children seemed to be using an order-of-mention strategy.

In summary, the results of the temporal order tasks indicate that children do not understand the temporal order function of the causal connectives until the age of about 7 or 8 at the earliest. There is also evidence to support the hypothesis that the younger children make use of an order-of-mention strategy. It is not totally clear whether these children actually believe that *because* (in sentence-medial position) is equivalent to *and then* or whether they are merely using the order-of-mention strategy as a means of organising their responses in particular types of experimental tasks. Emerson's finding that the order-of-mention effect was stronger for the FLT than for the PST suggests that the latter interpretation is more appropriate. Further evidence in support of this interpretation will be presented in Chapter 4. However, Emerson's claim that the children who use an order-of-mention strategy lack any knowledge of the directional element of the causal connectives' meaning will be challenged on the grounds that such knowledge may be based on causal direction rather than on temporal order.

(b) Causal direction tasks

In this section we shall consider some experiments which appear to test the child's knowledge of the causal connectives' function as indicators of causal direction. Epstein (1972) used a *Why*-response task which involved presenting 6- to 11-year-olds with a causal sentence and then asking a 'Did I tell you why...?' question about each clause. For example, the experimenter would say, 'The boy was happy because he got a cookie,' and would then ask, 'Did I tell you why he got a cookie?' and 'Did I tell you why he was happy?' Epstein found that the 6- to 7-year-olds and the 8- to 9-year-olds showed a strong tendency to answer 'Yes' to both questions in a pair. She interprets this as evidence in support of Piaget's claim that, for the young child, the elements in a causal relation are simply related by juxtaposition rather than being related in terms of some type of order or direction. However, the young children's performance may be attributable to a tendency to acquiesce. In particular, the children may believe that an adult would not ask an unanswerable *Why?* question, and therefore that they must have been given the information which would be required to answer the question. Another problem with Epstein's method arises from the fact that she used unacceptable sentences as well as acceptable sentences and that she trained the children to base their responses on the semantic plausibility cues. For example, for an unacceptable sentence such as:

(2.7) *The boy got a cookie because he was happy,

the children would be encouraged to respond 'Yes' to:

(2.8) *Did I tell you why he was happy?*

Yet, 'Yes' would also be the 'correct' response to this question for the corresponding acceptable sentence:

(2.9) *The boy was happy because he got a cookie.*

Thus, the experimenter created a confused and confusing context in which it might appear that 'anything goes'. This may have encouraged the children to conclude that a *because* sentence can provide an answer to any *Why?* question which is based on one of the sentence's clauses.

Roth (1980) administered a sentence completion task to 3- to 11-year-olds.[4] For each item, the child was presented with a sentence fragment of the form *Y because...* and also with two pictures. One of these pictures depicted an event which was temporally prior to Y and which would be likely to cause Y. The other picture depicted an event which was also temporally prior to Y but which was causally irrelevant. The child was asked to 'finish each story with the best ending for that story'. Roth found that the children in all the age groups consistently completed the sentence by referring to the causally related event, and that references to the event which was only temporally related to Y were extremely rare. Also, responses which involved references to a consequence rather than a cause of Y were very infrequent. Roth argues that this constitutes evidence that the children understood that *because* specifies the direction of the causal relation and that it introduces a cause rather than a consequence. However, the evidence is not very strong, since the children were not presented with a picture depicting a consequence and so would have had to invent a consequence, whereas they were presented with a 'ready-made' cause.

Corrigan (1975) also used a sentence completion task. She presented 3- to 7-year-olds with a simple sentence followed by an incomplete sentence ending with *because* and asked them to finish 'the story'. The simple sentence corresponded to the appropriate completion of the sentence fragment:

(2.10) *The boy threw a stone. The window broke because...*

As in her acceptability task, Corrigan included sentences expressing three types of relation (physical, affective and logical), and she found that the children's performance varied according to the type of relation. For instance, the affective items were passed by 90% of the 4-year-olds, and the physical items were passed by 90% of the 4-year-olds, and the physical items were passed by 90% of the 5-year-olds, whereas, on the logical items, only 55% of the 7-year-olds passed. Corrigan argues that success on the logical items can occur only when the child has reached Piaget's concrete operations stage, and she interprets her results as providing support for this argument. However, a methodological problem arises with respect to Corrigan's logical items. The example which Corrigan provides of a logical item is:

(2.11) *The cat meowed at the girl. The cat is alive because...*

In order to respond correctly, the children have to realise that they are being asked to justify the judgement that the cat is alive rather than to explain the fact that the cat is alive. In other words, they are being asked for an explanation in the deductive mode rather than the empirical mode. (See section 1.4.) However, the sentence fragment is not marked linguistically as being in the deductive mode. It can be regarded as an elliptical version of a sentence fragment like:

(2.12) *We know that the cat is alive because...*

Since the linguistic marking has been omitted in Corrigan's example, it is difficult to see how the children could have been expected to realise that they were being asked for a deductive explanation. The situation is further confused by the fact that, in Corrigan's acceptability task (which was administered to the same subjects), the children were expected to judge the following sentence as unacceptable:

(2.13) *Kathy was angry with Paul because she kicked him.*

There is no principled way of disallowing a deductive mode interpretation of this sentence while requiring a deductive mode interpretation of (2.11).

If we disregard the evidence from these problematic logical items, then Corrigan's findings indicate that 5-year-olds have some understanding of *because* and that even 4-year-olds perform very well when *because* is being used to express affective relations. However, like Roth's task, Corrigan's task is open to the criticism that the structure of the task is likely to have encouraged the children to refer to the cause in their completion of the sentence. Corrigan did include some control items for which the first sentence referred to an event which was unrelated to the event referred to in the sentence fragment (e.g. *Karen's toy broke. It is raining outside because...*). The fact that, on these items, very few of the children used the first sentence to complete the sentence fragment indicates that the children were not simply following a strategy of using the first sentence to complete the second sentence without taking account of the semantic relation between the sentences. Nevertheless, like Roth's results, Corrigan's results demonstrate only that the children know that it is better to follow *because* with a reference to a cause than with a reference to a causally irrelevant event. These results are not relevant to the hypothesis that young children know that *because* should be followed by a reference to a cause rather than an effect.

There is, to my knowledge, only one study involving a comprehension task which provides an adequate test of children's knowledge of the causal connectives' function as indicators of causal direction. This is a study by Trabasso, Stein and Johnson (1981)[5] in which 5-, 7- and 9-year-olds were asked to complete sentence fragments ending with *because*. The children in this experiment, unlike those in Roth's and Corrigan's experiments, were required to generate a cause for themselves since they were not presented with either a picture or a sentence corresponding to the cause. Thus, the structure of the task was not cueing the children in to referring to causes in their sentence completions. Although the frequency of appropriate responses showed a significant increase with age, even for the 5-year-olds 86% of the responses correctly referred to causes of the events mentioned in the sentence fragments. This finding indicates that 5-year-olds have some understanding of the causal connectives' function as indicators of causal direction: they know that *because* introduces a cause.

2.1.5 *Production experiments*

Several studies have aimed to elicit uses of the causal connectives from children. Sullivan (1972) asked 4- to 10-year-olds to tell stories about pairs of pictures, which depicted events which were either causally related or arbitrarily related. At the beginning of the session, the experimenter demonstrated the task by presenting an example picture-pair and producing a *Because X, Y* sentence which referred to the events depicted by the pictures. Then she asked the child, 'Can you tell me a story like that? Make sure that you tell a story about both of the pictures together.' Before each test item, the experimenter gave the child the instruction: 'Tell me a story about these two pictures.' Sullivan found that the frequency of use of the causal connectives was low at all the age levels studied. However, this result tells us only that Sullivan's elicitation technique was not successful. It does not allow us to conclude that the children were incapable of using causal connectives.

Katz and Brent (1968) investigated children's production of causal connectives by encouraging them to engage in free conversation and also by asking them to tell stories about sets of pictures. They found that the 6- to 7-year-olds and the 11- to 12-year-olds used *because* equally frequently, and that most of the uses involved psychological relations. The 6- to 7-year-olds did not produce any cause–effect inversions. Katz and Brent note that some of the

11- to 12-year-olds produced utterances which bore a superficial resemblance to inversions, but which could reasonably be interpreted as elliptical expressions in the deductive mode.

Kuhn and Phelps (1976) presented 5- to 8-year-olds with single pictures depicting causal sequences, and asked the children to 'say a sentence with *because* that tells about this picture'. The children were also asked to 'say a sentence with *because*' without the support of a visual stimulus. Only 2 (out of 68) children failed to produce any correct *because* sentences, and there were only eight instances of cause–effect inversions. It is difficult to calculate the proportion of the total uses of *because* which these inversions represent (since the data are not sufficiently detailed), but, even at the most conservative estimate, the inversion rate could not be more than about 4%. Thus, like Katz and Brent's results, these results indicate that the children were able to use *because* appropriately.

Similar findings were obtained by Trabasso, Stein and Johnson (1981). They presented 5-, 7- and 9-year-olds with sentences (which did not contain connectives), and after each sentence they asked the children to produce another sentence which would continue the story. Although the children did not always produce connectives, the results indicate that even the 5-year-olds were consistently correct when they did produce *because*.

The results of the production experiments demonstrate that children as young as 5 years are able to use *because* appropriately. This implies that even 5-year-olds have some knowledge of the directional element of the meaning of *because*.

2.1.6 *Observational studies of children's spontaneous production*

Several studies have charted the ages at which children begin to use the causal connectives and at which children appear to start trying to express causal relations in their spontaneous speech.

Limber (1973) collected spontaneous speech data from twelve English-speaking children, and found that the children began to use *because* and *so* between the ages of 2; 6 and 3; 0. Before that stage, the children either juxtaposed the clauses or linked them with *and*.

Clancy, Jacobsen and Silva (1976) studied the spontaneous speech of English-speaking, Italian-speaking, Turkish-speaking and German-speaking children with the aim of investigating when the notions underlying co-ordinate and subordinate constructions are acquired. Clancy *et al.* assumed that the child may be expressing such notions as coordination, temporal sequence or causality even when she does not mark them with an appropriate connective. Therefore, they used a rich interpretation method (based on the content and context of the child's utterances) to infer the notions which the child was trying to express. On this basis, they concluded that, for all of the four languages studied, some expressions of the notion of causality had occurred by the age of 2; 10.

Bloom *et al.* (1980) carried out a study which incorporated the aims of both Limber's study and Clancy *et al.*'s study, and which yielded similar findings. Bloom *et al.* made a longitudinal study of the spontaneous speech of four English-speaking children between the ages of 2; 0 and 3; 2. All the children had begun using *because* by the age of 2; 10. One of the children began using *so* before *because*, while the other three children used *because* first. Bloom *et al.* estimated that the children began to express causal relations between the ages of 2; 2 and 2; 7. Two of the children began expressing causal relations at about the same time as they began using causal connectives, whereas the other two children used *and* to express causal relations before they began using causal connectives. Bloom *et al.* also present some evidence which suggests that, before the age of 3; 2, the children were systematically using *because* to express causal relations, and that some of them were systematically using *so* to express causal relations.

Of course, the fact that very young children use causal connectives to express causal relations does not necessarily mean that they are taking account of the direction of the causal relation in their use of the connectives. Hood (1977)[6] assessed the occurrence of cause–effect inversions in young children's spontaneous speech. She carried out a longitudinal study of eight children between the ages of 2; 0 and 3; 5. (Four of these children were the children studied by Bloom *et al.* (1980).) Out of a total of 2,220 causally interpretable statements, 618 (28%) contained *because* and 310 (14%) contained *so*. Therefore, 42% of the causal relations were explicitly marked by a causal connective. When Hood examined the 928 uses of the causal connectives, she found that there were only 63 inversions. In other words, only 7% of the children's uses of the causal connectives were inverted. Most of the inversions involved *because*, but, even for *because*, the inversion rate was only 9%. Also, most of these *because* inversions were produced by one particular child, but, even for this child, the *because* inversions constituted only 16% of his total uses of *because*. Therefore, Hood's findings indicate that, even at the age of about $2\frac{1}{2}$ or 3 years, children systematically follow *because* with a cause rather than an effect. This implies that they do have some understanding of the directional element of the causal connectives' meaning.

Hood's study also produced some other interesting findings. She found that when the children were expressing causal relations, some of them used mainly the 'cause → effect' order, some used mainly the 'effect → cause' order, and some made approximately equal use of the two orders. These clause order preferences were evident even before the causal connectives first appeared. When the children did start using causal connectives, there was a tendency for each child to begin by using the connective which was consistent with her preferred clause order. For example, the children who used mainly the 'effect → cause' order began using *because* before *so*.

Hood also found that most of the causal relations which the children expressed were psychological rather than physical, but she points out that this is no reason for regarding the expressions as unsystematic. Piaget (1930) regards psychological relations as a primitive form of causality. However, the *linguistic* demands imposed by expressions of psychological causality are no less than those imposed by expressions of physical causality. In addition, Hood notes that most of the children's causal statements referred to intentions or were requests for action, and that they often referred to negative situations (such as the non-occurrence of an event). There was also a strong tendency for the causal utterances to refer to ongoing or immediately future events or states, rather than to past events or events in the more distant future.

Thus, Hood's evidence suggests that early expressions of causality may be restricted in their semantic content, but that, within this limited realm, even $2\frac{1}{2}$- to 3-year-olds demonstrate an ability to make a systematically correct distinction between cause and effect when they use causal connectives in their spontaneous speech.

McCabe and Peterson (1985) extended Hood's study by using a larger sample and an older age group (3- to 9-year-olds). The children were asked to talk to the researcher about various personal experiences. (McCabe and Peterson imply that the situation was relatively unstructured, so it seems reasonable to class their study as 'observational' rather than 'experimental'.) As in Hood's study, cause–effect inversions were found to be very rare. No age trend was obtained since even the 3-year-olds were using the causal connectives appropriately. The results also confirmed Hood's finding that most of the children's uses of the connectives involved expressions of psychological relations. The main difference between the two sets of results is that McCabe and Peterson's subjects talked mainly about the past, whereas Hood's subjects talked mainly about the present and the immediate future. McCabe and Peterson argue that this difference in results reflects a developmental shift. However, the difference might be attributable to a procedural difference in that McCabe and Peterson seem to have been encouraging their subjects to reminisce about past experiences.

The evidence from observational studies of children's production indicates that children are capable of using the causal connectives appropriately from the age of $2\frac{1}{2}$ years. Thus, it seems that some knowledge of the connectives' directionality is present at a very early age, although this knowledge may be restricted to expressions of psychological causality.

2.2 Children's understanding of causality

2.2.1 *The precausality debate*

Piaget (1929, 1930) claims that children do not have a true understanding of causality until about the age of 7 or 8 years, and that before this age their thinking about causal phenomena is precausal. Piaget (1930:267) defines precausality as 'the confusion of relations of a psychological or biological type in general with relations of a mechanical type'. According to Piaget, young children's view of causality is subjective rather than objective. They do not distinguish between themselves and the universe, and so they do not distinguish between motivation and physical causality. They view the physical world in the same way as the social world, and they believe that both can be explained in terms of psychological motivation. Piaget identifies nine types of precausal relation, and he says that they all 'appeal either to motives or to intentions, either to occult emanations or to mystical manufactures'. Piaget's claims about precausality have their roots in his writings on children's understanding of the causal connectives (see section 2.1.1), where he argued that children tend to convert physical and logical relations into psychological relations. However, the main evidence which Piaget uses to support his argument about the precausal nature of early thought comes from a series of experiments in which he asked children to explain a range of phenomena, such as dreams, the origin of the sun and moon, the weather, the nature of air, the movement of the clouds, the floating of boats, and the workings of a steam-engine. As one would expect, young children do not give explanations of these phenomena which are correct from the point of view of modern scientific knowledge. However, Piaget's thesis is not simply that the young child's explanations are incorrect, but that they provide evidence for the precausal nature of early thought.

This claim has been challenged by a number of authors (e.g. Deutsche, 1937; Huang, 1943; Berzonsky, 1971; Roth, 1980), who have argued that early thought is not characteristically precausal, but that young children may resort to precausal types of explanation when they are asked to explain unfamiliar phenomena or phenomena with opaque causal mechanisms. In more favourable circumstances, the children will give physical types of explanations of physical phenomena. For instance, Huang (1943) found that when he presented 4- to 10-year-olds with simple demonstrations in which a physical law was violated, most of the explanations were of a physical character. Many of these explanations were scientifically incorrect in that they appealed to simple principles, like pushing or blocking, rather than to the principles used in physics, such as surface tension or centrifugal force.

However, as Huang points out, these 'naive physical explanations' have much in common with the explanations used by the adult layman.

In defending Piaget's thesis, Laurendeau and Pinard (1962) make two main points about the evidence presented by Piaget's critics. First, they argue that this evidence is based on an over-narrow interpretation of Piaget's term 'precausal thought'. In a sense, this criticism is justified in that Piaget's critics probably tend to class most explanations which overtly appeal to physical forces and not to psychological forces as naturalistic. For Piaget, on the other hand, an explanation can be classed as showing the characteristics of precausal thought even if it does not explicitly refer to psychological causes. For instance, here is one of Piaget's examples of a precausal explanation of the origin of wind and breath:

MON (7): Blow. What happens when you blow? –
Air. – Where does it come from? – *From outside.* –
– Is there air in the room? – *No.* – Inside you?
– *No.* – In your mouth? – *Yes.* – Where does it come from? – *From outside.* –
How did it come? –...– How did it get inside you? – *Through the mouth.* (1930:54)

The following quotation provides an illustration of Piaget's interpretation of such explanations:

But it should be emphasised once more that this drawing in of wind by breathing is more in the nature of participation than of attraction. In other words, the child does not imagine that we are mere receptacles for the outside air. We make air ourselves. Not only do Roy, Taq, and the rest attribute a human origin to the air out of doors, but all our children stress the point that we can make air ourselves whenever we want to...We have here participation between two autonomous wills, and not mechanical action of one on the other. If we take the children's ideas as a whole, it will be easy enough to find the right mental context for their statements. (1930:55)

It would be just as reasonable to argue that Piaget is over-interpreting the children's explanations as to argue that Piaget's critics are working with too narrow a definition of 'precausal thought'!

Laurendeau and Pinard's second point is related to the final sentence of the above quotation from Piaget. They note that there is a fundamental difference between the method of analysis used by Piaget and that used by most of his critics. Piaget used a global method which consists of 'the global evaluation of all the child's answers to a group of problems, all aiming at the determination of the presence or absence of a certain type of primitive thinking' (Laurendeau and Pinard, 1962:31). In contrast, Piaget's critics usually employed a much more analytical technique which involves computing the frequency of precausal responses given for each item. Laurendeau and Pinard argue that the analytical technique is less valid than the global technique, since it fails to take account of the children's justifications of their responses and since it fails to provide an overall picture of the child's performance on the test. However, the global technique could also be criticised because of its impressionistic nature. The global technique certainly enabled Piaget to produce a fascinating and coherent account of the development of causality, but it has probably resulted in the extent and significance of precausal thought being over-emphasised.

2.2.2 *The notion of 'plausible cause'*

One of the types of precausal relation which Piaget identifies is that of phenomenistic causality in which 'two facts given together in perception, and such that no relation subsists between them except that of contiguity in time and space, are regarded as being connected by a relation of causality' (1930:259). Piaget sums up the characteristics of phenomenistic causality by claiming that, for the young child: 'Anything may produce anything.'

This claim, like most of Piaget's other claims regarding precausality, has not gone unchallenged. Indeed, there is a considerable body of evidence which indicates that young children have a good understanding of the constraints governing causal relations. Young children do not believe that anything may produce anything. Instead, they have some knowledge as to what constitutes a 'plausible cause' for a given effect.

Much of the recent research into children's understanding of causality concerns the three general causal principles of temporal precedence, covariation and contiguity. (For a useful review of this research, see Sedlak and Kurtz, 1981.) These three principles state, respectively, that a cause is temporally prior to its effect, that a cause covaries systematically with its effect, and that a cause is contiguous with its effect in place and time.

Evidence that young children understand temporal precedence comes from studies by Shultz and Mendelson (1975), Kun (1978) and Bullock and Gelman (1979). In Bullock and Gelman's study, children received a 'Jack-in-the-Box' task in which they observed a sequence of three physical events (a ball being dropped down one runway into the box, the jack jumping, and a ball being dropped down the other runway into the box). Even 3-year-olds consistently selected the prior event as the cause of the jack jumping, despite the fact that the events were novel and despite the fact that there were no pragmatic constraints making the prior event a more plausible cause than the subsequent event. Furthermore, this preference for the prior event persisted when a conflict was introduced between temporal precedence and spatial contiguity. On the other hand, Sophian and Huber (1984) found that in a more complex situation involving several alternative cues 3-year-olds did not consistently rely on the temporal precedence cue, whereas 5-year-olds did systematically choose prior events as causes. Thus, the evidence indicates that

3-year-olds can make use of temporal precedence cues although they sometimes weight other cues more highly, and that by the age of 6 years children are relatively consistent in their adherence to the temporal precedence principle.

A similar conclusion can be drawn regarding children's understanding of the covariation principle. The composite results from studies by Shultz and Mendelson (1975), Siegler and Liebert (1974), and Siegler (1975, 1976) indicate that 3-year-olds are capable of selecting the consistently covarying event as the cause in simple situations, but that it is not until the children are older (about 8 years) that they are able to make systematic use of the covariation principle in more complex situations.

Evidence regarding children's understanding of spatial and temporal contiguity cues comes mainly from studies which have aimed to assess the relative importance of contiguity cues as opposed to other cues. As mentioned earlier, Bullock and Gelman (1979) found that children tend to ignore spatial contiguity cues when these conflict with temporal precedence. On the other hand, there is some evidence to suggest that when the conflict is between contiguity and covariation cues, young children tend to respond on the basis of the contiguity cues (Siegler and Liebert, 1974; Siegler, 1975; Mendelson and Shultz, 1976). This evidence indicates that, at least by the age of 4 years, children prefer causes to be spatially and temporally contiguous (rather than non-contiguous) with their effects. Indeed, recent research by Leslie (1982, 1984) suggests that even 7-month-old infants are sensitive to spatial and temporal contiguity cues in their perception of simple causal events.

The principles of temporal precedence, covariation and contiguity can all be regarded as relating to the general 'structure' of causal events. There is a further body of research which examines children's understanding of the 'content relations' between causes and effects. Again, the evidence indicates that young children do not believe that anything can cause anything.

One constraint which children observe in their causal reasoning is that causes should be similar to their effects. Huang, Yang and Yao (1945) presented 4- to 9-year-olds with a demonstration in which a piece of litmus paper changed colour when it was moved from one beaker of liquid to another. In one condition (the 'colour similar' condition), each beaker was placed on a piece of cardboard which was the same colour as the colour which the litmus paper changed to when placed in that beaker. In another condition (the 'colour dissimilar' condition), the two pieces of cardboard varied in size but not in colour, and the colour did not correspond to either of the colours of the litmus paper. Huang *et al.* found that 82% of the subjects in the colour similar condition attributed the litmus paper's colour change to the effect of the cardboard, whereas only 9% of the subjects in the colour dissimilar condition did so. Therefore, Huang *et al.* conclude that similarity is a powerful factor in determining causal attribution.

Shultz and Ravinsky (1977) draw a similar conclusion. They found that 6- to 12-year-olds were more likely to attribute an effect to a similar cause than to a dissimilar cause. For example, when three lights came on, the children were more likely to conclude that a triple switch had been pressed than to conclude that a single switch had been pressed. However, Shultz and Ravinsky found that similarity was not the only principle which affected the children's judgements. When the similarity principle conflicted with the principle of covariation or temporal contiguity, the children tended to abandon the similarity principle, and this tendency increased with age.

Research has also shown that young children have some understanding of the mechanisms which underlie certain specific causal events. For example, Bullock (1984) investigated children's knowledge that two objects which are pushing or pulling one another must be linked by some connecting mechanism. She assessed the children's understanding by using a variety of response modes (e.g. showing surprise at an apparent lack of mechanism; giving an explanation of a possible mechanism), and she found that 5-year-olds were consistent in demonstrating an understanding of mechanism across all the response modes. However, even 3-year-olds showed some awareness of the need for a connecting mechanism in that they expressed surprise when two objects moved in tandem without any apparent connecting mechanism.

Keil (1979) assessed $1\frac{1}{2}$- and $2\frac{1}{2}$-year-olds' knowledge of the causal mechanism governing the collapse or non-collapse of physical structures. In particular, he investigated whether children were surprised by 'trick' trials which violated the physical laws of balance and support. The results indicated that both age groups had an understanding of the law of support but that neither age group understood the law of balance. Thus, children as young as $1\frac{1}{2}$ years know that there is a causal relation between lack of support and collapse of physical structures.

Shultz (1982) argues that young children interpret causal events in generative rather than empiricist terms. In other words, they believe that causes actually generate or produce their effects and therefore that causal connections are necessary as opposed to coincidental. Young children's understanding of causality does not correspond to the empiricist doctrine that causes and effects are independent events which merely become associated in the observer's mind because of their covariation and their spatio-temporal contiguity. Shultz's argument receives considerable support from the findings indicating that young children expect causes to be similar to their effects and that young children have some understanding of causal mechanisms.

Overall, recent research into children's understanding of causality has yielded a very promising picture of young children's ability. Even at the age of 3 years, children can distinguish between causes and effects and have some understanding as to what would constitute a plausible cause for a given effect. This picture of young children's competence in the cognitive domain contrasts sharply with the picture of lack of competence in the linguistic domain created by most previous studies of children's comprehension of the causal connectives. It is of course possible that this is an area where linguistic development lags behind cognitive development: children might understand causal relations without knowing how these relations are encoded linguistically by the causal connectives. However, the extent of the apparent lag (about 5 years) is rather surprising, especially in view of the fact that young children do produce causal connectives. In subsequent chapters, I shall present evidence which indicates that this discrepancy between cognition and language (like the discrepancy between the comprehension and production of the causal connectives) is more apparent than real and arises mainly because previous comprehension experiments have tended to under-estimate children's knowledge of the causal connectives' meaning. Furthermore, I shall be arguing that a major reason for this under-estimation is that comprehension experiments have typically relied too heavily on assessing use of the temporal precedence principle. The research reviewed in this section demonstrates that young children's concept of 'plausible cause' is complex and includes much more than just the knowledge that causes generally precede their effects. Young children's concept of plausible cause also includes knowledge about covariation, about spatial and temporal contiguity, about cause–effect similarity, and about the causal mechanisms which enable causes to produce their effects. In addition, the evidence reviewed in section 2.2.1 suggests that young children know that a plausible cause for a physical phenomenon has to be physical rather than psychological. Further support for this claim is provided by the elicited production studies to which we now turn.

3   Elicited production studies

3.1 Introduction

Most of the previous studies involving causal connectives can be criticised on the grounds that they may be imposing demands on the children which are extraneous to the demands faced when comprehending or producing causal connectives in normal discourse. Two notable exceptions to this are the studies by Hood (1977) and by McCabe and Peterson (1985). In these naturalistic studies of children's language production, cause–effect inversions were found to be extremely rare even for the youngest children (2- to 3-year-olds). On the other hand, both studies found that most of the children's uses of the causal connectives involved psychological relations rather than physical or logical relations. This led the authors to propose that one possible explanation for the discrepancy between their results and those of most of the other studies (which suggest that children do not understand the causal connectives until the age of about 7 or 8) would be that the ability to use and understand causal connectives appropriately is initially restricted to expressions with psychological content. In production studies, children can choose to talk about psychological content and will therefore appear competent in their use of *because* and *so*. Comprehension studies, on the other hand, typically include physical and/or logical content in addition to psychological content, so they will tend to reveal any limitations in children's knowledge of the connectives' meaning. Thus, the work of Hood and of McCabe and Peterson suggests an interesting hypothesis as to how the discrepant results might be explained. However, this hypothesis (that knowledge of the causal connectives' meaning is initially restricted to psychological content) cannot be tested on the basis of data from spontaneous production studies. The fact that the children *did not* express many physical or logical relations does not necessarily mean that they *could not* do so.

One way of testing the 'psychological content' hypothesis would be to encourage young children to talk about non-psychological phenomena (as well as psychological phenomena) and then assess their use of causal expressions. This is the approach adopted in the studies reported in this chapter. These studies made use of a loosely structured interview technique to elicit explanations and justifications of several types of phenomenon from nursery school children. The elicited production method represents a compromise between the experimental and observational approaches, in that it enables the researcher to exercise some control over the content of the child's utterances without making the task very constrained.

The results of the elicited production studies will be used to address three main questions:

(1) To what extent do the children produce cause–effect inversions?
(2) Does the inversion rate vary according to the type of phenomenon which is being explained?
(3) Do the children give appropriate explanations for the different types of phenomenon?

Conflicting predictions regarding these three questions can be derived from the existing literature.

Hood's and McCabe and Peterson's findings would lead one to predict that cause–effect inversions will be rare. However, these authors also suggest that this prediction might be restricted to psychological relations; and their proposed explanation for the discrepancy between their results and those of the other studies would predict that when young children are required to express physical or logical relations, they will tend either to produce inversions or to 'psychologise' by inappropriately converting the physical or logical relations into psychological relations.

Piaget argues that young children think *because* and *so* refer to causal relations which are undifferentiated with respect to causal direction. Since Piaget gives us no reason to suppose that children will systematically favour either one of the cause–effect orders, his theory would presumably predict that for young children the frequency of inversions will be approximately equal to the frequency of correct uses of the causal connectives. The results of those experiments which have employed either metalinguistic tasks or comprehension tasks based on temporal order would also lead one to make this prediction. Like Hood, Piaget predicts that children will be able to deal with psychological relations before they can deal with physical or logical relations. However, he probably would not predict that children as young as those studied here would systematically use the causal connectives appropriately even when the content was psychological. Therefore, Piaget's theory would not necessarily predict variations in the inversion rate according to the type of phenomenon. On the other hand, Piaget's theory does yield a clear prediction as far as the third question is concerned. Piaget regards the tendency to psychologise as one of the characteristics of precausal thought, so he predicts that young children's explanations of physical and logical phenomena will frequently be inappropriate. However, some other researchers, such as Deutsche (1937) and

Table 2. *Mean age and age range of subjects in elicited production studies*

	3- to 4-year-olds		4- to 5-year-olds	
	Mean	Range	Mean	Range
Experiment 1	3;5	3;2 to 3;10	4;8	4;6 to 4;11
Experiment 2	3;6	3;3 to 3;11	4;9	4;7 to 4;11
Experiment 3	3;8	3;4 to 4;0	4;11	4;9 to 5;1

Huang (1943) (see section 2.2.1), would predict that the children's explanations would be appropriate (at least when they were explaining physical or psychological phenomena).

Given the variety of expectations about nursery school children's capacity in this area, it is clearly important to explore it further.

3.2 Method

3.2.1 *General*

All the subjects received three tasks. One involved explaining a physical phenomenon, one a psychological phenomenon, and one a logical or rule-based phenomenon. There was always an interval of several weeks between tasks, and the tasks were presented in the order: physical, psychological, logical.

All the subjects were attending the Psychology Department Nursery of the University of Edinburgh. There were eight subjects in each of two age groups: 3- to 4-year-olds and 4- to 5-year-olds. The details of the subjects' ages at the time of each experiment are presented in Table 2. The younger group consisted of two girls and six boys, and the older group consisted of four girls and four boys. Each subject was tested individually. The sessions were video-taped, and then transcribed. The procedures used in each of the three experiments are summarised below, but further details are given in Appendix 1.

3.2.2 *Procedure for Experiment 1: Ker Plunk (physical)*

The 'physical' experiment made use of the materials from a commercially produced game, Ker Plunk. These consist of a vertical plastic tube down which marbles can be dropped, and a set of plastic sticks which can be inserted horizontally in such a way that they partially block the cavity and prevent the marbles from falling. (See Figure 1.) In the first phase of the experiment, the experimenter demonstrated the relations of physical causality associated with the apparatus. First, the tube was presented without any sticks in, and

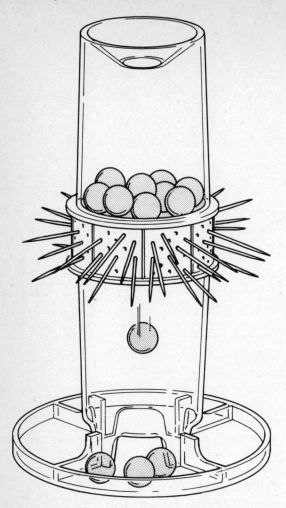

Figure I: Materials used in Ker Plunk experiment

some marbles were dropped into the tube. Then the sticks were inserted, and the marbles were dropped on to the sticks. Next, some sticks which were not supporting any marbles were removed. Finally some sticks which were supporting marbles were removed and the marbles fell. Throughout the demonstration, the child was encouraged to offer suggestions, predictions, descriptions and explanations. At certain points, the child was also encouraged to take part in inserting the marbles and in inserting or removing the sticks. In the second phase of the experiment, a large toy panda called Choo-Choo was introduced, and the child was asked to tell him how to play with the toy.

Happy   Sad   Happy   Sad

Cross   Scared   Cross   Scared

Figure 2: Materials used in Facial Expressions experiment

3.2.3 *Procedure for Experiment 2: Facial Expressions (psychological)*

In the 'psychological' experiment, the child's task was to explain why a character was experiencing a particular emotion. The materials consisted of two cardboard cut-out dolls (a boy and a girl), and two sets of four schematic faces showing different facial expressions: happy, sad, cross and scared. (See Figure 2.) These faces could be attached to the dolls, and could be interchanged. The girls were shown only the girl doll, and the boys were shown only the boy doll. At the beginning of the session, the experimenter attached each face to the doll in turn, and named the facial expressions for the child. Once the child had been introduced to the materials, the experimenter put one of the faces on the doll, named the facial expression, and asked the child to tell a little story about the doll. If necessary, the experimenter asked more directive questions, such as 'Why is Jack sad?'. The procedure was repeated until all four facial expressions had been presented (in a random order).[1]

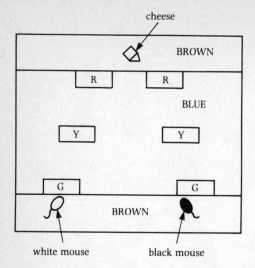

R = red stepping-stone

Y = yellow stepping-stone

G = green stepping-stone

Figure 3: Materials used in Game with Rules experiment

3.2.4 *Procedure for Experiment 3: Game with Rules (logical)*

The 'logical' experiment involved a board game with arbitrary rules, in which two players threw a coloured die and raced toy mice over coloured stepping-stones to a piece of cheese. (See Figure 3.) There were three colours on the die: red, yellow and green. These colours corresponded to the colours of the stepping-stones. The experimenter began by introducing the child to the materials and stating the rules of the game:

(1) The colour on the die has to be the same as the colour of the stepping-stone for you to put your mouse on the stepping-stone.

(2) The mice must stay on the stepping-stones. They must not go into the water.

(3) The mice must jump on to all the stepping-stones. They must not miss out any stepping-stones.

Then the experimenter played the game twice with the subject, correcting any mistakes the subject made and re-stating the relevant rules. After this training phase, the toy panda used in the Ker Plunk experiment was produced again, and the child was asked to tell Choo-Choo how to play the game. Finally, the child was asked to play the game with Choo-Choo and to tell him if he made a mistake. The experimenter made the moves for Choo-Choo and ensured that Choo-Choo made several mistakes in each game. If the child detected a mistake, the experimenter asked the child to tell Choo-Choo why he was wrong and to correct him.

3.3 Analysis of results

The first stage in analysing the results involved dividing the transcripts into propositions, and making lists of the pairs of adjacent propositions between which a relation could potentially hold. Propositions were included in the list irrespective of whether the potential relation was causal or not, and irrespective of whether the clauses were linked by a connective of juxtaposed. The connectives which did occur in the original transcripts were omitted when the lists were constructed. Propositions which had been expressed by the experimenter were included where there was a potential relation between the proposition expressed by the experimenter and a proposition expressed by the child. For example, if the experimenter said 'Why is Jack sad?', and the child then said 'Because he's hurt his leg,' then the following pair of propositions would be included in the list:

Jack is sad → Jack has hurt his leg.

As this example illustrates, tense markers were not eliminated from the propositions.

Then the lists of propositions and the original transcripts were laid aside for a week. This was done in an attempt to eliminate the effect of the connectives on the subsequent coding.[2]

After a week had passed, each pair of propositions was coded according to the type of relation which seemed to hold between the two propositions. The coding categories are listed and defined in Table 3. In many cases, the most convenient way of defining a category is in terms of the connective which would be used to express the relation. However, there is not a one-to-one correspondence between the connectives and the relations.

Sometimes there was more than one potential relation between the two propositions. In such cases, the convention of always selecting the 'most complex' relation was adopted. For example, if it was not clear whether a relation was conjunctive or temporal, it was coded as temporal; or, if it was not clear whether a relation was causal or temporal, it was coded as causal. Therefore, it is probable that some of the relations which are coded as causal were not intended to be causal.

Two further analyses were carried out on the relations which had been

Table 3. *Coding categories for elicited production data*

	Category	Definition/description
(i)	∅	There is no plausible relation between the propositions.
(ii)	tautological	Both propositions have the same content.
(iii)	conjunctive	There is some common topic between the propositions ('and').
(iv)	disjunctive	One proposition is an alternative to the other ('or').
(v)	opposition	An expectation is being countered ('but', 'although').
(vi)	instantiation	The second proposition provides an example or illustration of the generalisation expressed by the first proposition.
(vii)	temporal	There is a sequential relation between the events/states referred to by the propositions ('then', 'first').
(viii)	simultaneous	The two propositions refer to events/states which happened at the same time ('while').
(ix)	means	One proposition expresses a means of achieving the event/state referred to by the other proposition ('by', responses to 'How?').
(x)	intentional	The second proposition expresses the aim or purpose behind the action referred to in the first proposition ('to').
(xi)	causal	There is a relation of physical or psychological causality or of logical deduction between the events/states/concepts referred to by the propositions.

assigned to the causal category. First, the causal relations were coded for directionality. If the first proposition to be expressed referred to the cause, the relation was coded as 'C → E'. If the first proposition referred to the effect, the relation was coded as 'E → C'. If both directions seemed equally possible, the relation was coded as 'ambiguous'. Second, the relations were coded as physical, psychological or logical. (See section 1.3.)

Once all the codings had been made, the original transcripts were examined in conjunction with the coded lists of propositions. In this way, it was possible to explore the relationship between the use of the connectives and the type of relation between the propositions. In particular, for the relations in the causal category, it was possible to assess the frequency of cause–effect inversions. An inversion was said to occur if there was a clash between the causal direction coding and the causal direction specified by the connective. Therefore any of the following pairings would be counted as an inversion:

C → E + sentence-medial *because* (e.g. **John threw a ball at the window because the window broke*).

C → E + sentence-medial *if* (e.g. **You pass the exam if you get a certificate*).

C → E + sentence-medial *when* (e.g. **You pass the exam when you get a certificate*).

E → C + sentence-medial *so* (e.g. ** The window broke so John threw a ball at the window*).

> E → C + sentence-medial *that's why* (e.g. **The window broke – that's why John threw a ball at the window*).
>
> E → C + sentence-initial *because* (e.g. **Because the window broke, John threw a ball at the window*).
>
> E → C + sentence-initial *if* (e.g. **If you get a certificate, you pass the exam*).
>
> E → C + sentence-initial *when* (e.g. **When you get a certificate, you pass the exam*).

Those utterances which would be acceptable if they were regarded as elliptical deductive expressions (e.g. *She is cross because she has got big eyebrows*) were counted as inversions. In addition, those relations which had been coded as ambiguous in directionality were assumed to be inversions. Therefore, if anything, this method of analysis will tend to over-estimate the frequency of inversions.

The responses in the intentional category were also categorised as inverted or non-inverted. However, the method of detecting inversions was rather different from that used for the causal category. To determine whether or not an intentional response was inverted, it was necessary to examine the relationship between the connective and the syntactic structure of the second clause. For example, if the connective was *because* and the second clause contained the modal form *would* (as in *I pulled out the sticks because the marbles would fall*), then this was counted as an inversion. On the other hand, if the connective had been *so*, then the utterance would have been non-inverted.

3.4 Results

3.4.1 *Success in eliciting causal expressions*

Before addressing the main issues, it will be useful to consider the extent to which the children expressed causal relations and the extent to which they used the causal connectives. For this purpose, the intentional responses will be counted as causal. As Table 4 indicates, approximately half of the relations fall into the causal category. Of course, this may be an over-estimate, given the procedure which was used for deciding between alternative codings. Nevertheless, these results do suggest that the tasks provided reasonably natural contexts for the production of causal expressions. The low frequency of causal relations for the younger group in the Facial Expressions experiment is probably due to the fact that the task required a relatively high level of imagination and inventiveness. In many cases, the younger children gave 'don't know' responses.

Table 5 provides a general picture of the children's use of the causal connectives, and it reveals that *because* was used much more frequently than

Table 4. *Relations in causal category as frequencies and as percentages of total number of relations*[a]

	3 to 4 years		4 to 5 years		Total	
	f	%	f	%	f	%
Ker Plunk	96	53	173	54	269	53
Facial Expressions	31	76	102	47	133	52
Game with Rules	95	60	185	70	280	66
Total	222	58	460	57	682	58

[a] Causal includes intentional.

any of the other connectives. These results indicate that the tasks were relatively successful in eliciting causal connectives.

As can be seen from comparing Tables 4 and 5, there is not an exact correspondence between the causal relations and the causal connectives. The relations which were coded as causal were not always marked by a causal connective. In Table 6 the causal relations are categorised according to whether they were explicitly marked (by a causal connective), implicitly marked (by a connective such as *and* which implies a causal relation), juxtaposed (where there is no connective) or 'other' (where there is a connective which neither expresses nor implies a causal relation). The results indicate that, for both age groups and for all the tasks, the majority of the causal relations were explicitly marked as causal by the use of a causal connective. The results also provide some evidence for the existence of the phenomenon of juxtaposition. However, in the absence of comparable adult data, it is difficult to evaluate the significance of the juxtaposition percentages. It is also important to remember that the coding procedure used here will tend to over-estimate the frequency of juxtaposition.

It is interesting to compare the C → E relations with the E → C relations regarding the occurrence of explicit marking and of juxtaposition. The results presented in Table 7 indicate that the percentage of relations which were explicitly marked was always higher for the E → C relations than for the C → E relations. Conversely, the occurrence of juxtaposition was usually greater for the C → E relations than for the E → C relations. (The only exception to this was for the younger group's performance in the Facial Expressions experiment.) In a sense, these differences between the C → E and E → C relations are also likely to be due to the coding procedure, in that C → E relations are often ambiguous between a causal and a temporal interpretation, whereas E → C relations are less ambiguous. Therefore, some of the C → E relations which were not explicitly marked may actually be temporal relations which have

Table 5. *Frequency of causal connectives*

	Ker Plunk		Facial Expressions		Game with Rules		Totals		
	3 to 4	4 to 5	3 to 4	4 to 5	3 to 4	4 to 5	3 to 4	4 to 5	Both ages
– so –	8	8	1	17	19	40	28	65	93
–that's why –	1	0	2	3	0	2	3	5	8
if –	10	11	0	2	12	18	22	31	53
when –	1	10	0	5	1	7	2	22	24
– because –	65	123	20	47	30	68	115	238	353
– if –	1	5	0	0	1	2	2	7	9
–when –	2	6	0	0	1	7	3	13	16
– to –	3	3	1	2	0	0	4	5	9
Total	91	166	24	76	64	144	179	386	565

Table 6. *Percentage of causal relations which are explicitly marked (E),
implicitly marked (I), juxtaposed (J) or 'other' (O)*

	3 to 4 years				4 to 5 years				Total			
	E	I	J	O	E	I	J	O	E	I	J	O
Ker Plunk	66	11	22	1	79	12	9	0	74	12	13	1
Facial Expressions	65	13	22	0	58	11	31	0	59	11	29	0
Game with Rules	52	3	44	1	65	7	26	1	61	6	32	1
Total	59	8	32	1	69	10	21	0	66	9	24	1

Table 7. *Comparison between C → E and E → C with respect to the percentage
of relations which are explicitly marked or juxtaposed*

	Explicitly marked		Juxtaposed	
	C → E	E → C	C → E	E → C
3 to 4 years				
Ker Plunk	53	79	29	15
Facial Expressions	58	71	17	28
Game with Rules	40	77	53	23
Total	46	77	41	20
4 to 5 years				
Ker Plunk	50	92	18	4
Facial Expressions	30	80	48	18
Game with Rules	55	79	33	18
Total	48	85	32	12
Grand total	48	83	35	14

been 'over-interpreted' by the coding procedure. However, this difference in
ambiguity may reflect a more fundamental difference between C → E and
E → C relations. The C → E order may be the natural order for giving a
description, whereas the E → C order may be the natural order for giving an
explanation. If this were the case, then one would expect that causal direction
information would be expressed more explicitly when the order is E → C than
when it is C → E. (This point will be developed further in section 4.1.2.)
Whatever the explanation of the difference between the two types of relation,
the relatively high level of explicit marking for the E → C relations is of
interest in itself, as evidence that young children can and frequently do make
causal relations explicit rather than simply juxtaposing causally related

Table 8. *Occurrence of inversions: expressed as proportions and as percentages of number of explicitly marked causal relations*

	3 to 4 years		4 to 5 years		Total	
Ker Plunk	7/63	11%	9/137	6%	16/200	8%
Facial Expressions	6/20	30%	1/59	2%	7/79	9%
Game with Rules	1/49	2%	2/121	2%	3/170	2%
Total	14/132	11%	12/317	4%	26/449	6%

statements. Juxtapositions do occur, but, as Piaget himself points out, juxtapositions are not totally absent even from adults' speech.

3.4.2 *Frequency of inversions*

As Table 8 shows, the results fail to support Piaget's prediction that young children will tend to produce just as many inversions as correct uses of the causal connectives. The inversion rates are all considerably lower than 50%: with one exception, they are between only 2% and 11%. (The 30% inversion rate for the 3- to 4-year-olds in the Facial Expressions experiment should be interpreted with caution, since the corpus was so small.) Like Hood's and McCabe and Peterson's results, these results suggest that the young child does have some basis for understanding the directional component of the causal connectives' meaning.

3.4.3 *Relation between inversion rate and content*

When the inversion rates for the three experiments are compared (see Table 8), there is no evidence that the inversion rate varies according to the type of phenomenon being explained. Of course, this does not necessarily mean that the nature of the phenomenon never has any effect on the child's performance. What it does mean, though, is that the young child's ability to use causal connectives appropriately is not restricted to one content area (that of psychological phenomena) as Hood suggested it might be.

3.4.4 *Appropriateness of explanations*

If the children's explanations are appropriate, then there should be a close match between the nature of the phenomenon being explained and the type of relations expressed. More specifically, in the Ker Plunk experiment most of the utterances should express relations of physical causality, in the Facial Expressions experiment they should express relations of psychological caus-

Table 9. *Types of causal relation (physical/psychological/logical): expressed as frequencies and as percentages of the total number of explicitly marked causal relations for a given age group in a given experiment*

	Physical		Psychological		Logical	
	f	%	*f*	%	*f*	%
3 to 4 years						
Ker Plunk	47	75	13	21	3	5
Facial Expressions	0	0	19	95	1	5
Game with Rules	0	0	3	6	46	94
4 to 5 years						
Ker Plunk	92	67	29	21	16	12
Facial Expressions	2	3	55	93	2	3
Game with Rules	2	2	24	20	95	78

ality, and in the Game with Rules experiment they should express logical relations. If, on the other hand, the young child has a strong tendency to psychologise, expressions of psychological relations should predominate for all three types of phenomenon. The results presented in Table 9 provide evidence that, on the whole, the children's explanations were appropriate to the type of phenomenon. (Only relations which were explicitly marked as causal were included in this analysis.) The largest percentage for each row and for each column in Table 9 is in bold type. In every case, the percentage in bold type occurs in the cell where the type of phenomenon matches the type of relation.

On the other hand, the results also indicate that the children sometimes used psychological relations in the experiments involving physical and logical phenomena. At first sight, this may suggest that the children were psychologising. However, a closer examination of the actual utterances reveals that this is an over-simplification. For example, in the Ker Plunk experiment, when children expressed a psychological relation, they were often explaining their own actions rather than explaining physical events. Therefore, the expression of psychological relations was entirely appropriate. Moreover, the relations which were coded as 'psychological' were not always purely psychological. The child's action was often part of a sequence of physical causality, and the child's explanation of such an action usually implied an underlying knowledge of the physical relations. Here is an example of an utterance in which the expression of a psychological relation is appropriate and implies an underlying relation of physical causality:

Experimenter: *Tell Choo-Choo why we're putting the sticks in, will you?*
Angus (4;6): *Yes. Because we don't want them [the marbles] to make a loud clatter.*[3]

Discussion

There were only four clear instances of psychologising in the Ker Plunk experiment. The following example illustrates this inappropriate use of psychological relations:

Simon (4;7):   *They [the marbles] didn't go through.*
Experimenter: *Ah. I wonder why not.*
Simon: *'Cos they didn't want to.*

The situation is similar for the Game with Rules experiment. Sometimes the child expressed a psychological relation when he was explaining an action, as in:

Angus: *I just dropped it out, so I'll have another go.*
                        (The die had fallen out of the cup while Angus was shaking it.)

Also, the child sometimes invoked notions of 'fairness' and 'naughtiness', as in:

Experimenter: *Am I allowed to move it to the red? Yes?*
Andrew (4;11):   *No.*
Experimenter: *No? Why not?*
Andrew: *'Cos that isn't fair because he gets first to the cheese.*

In such cases, it is not clear whether the relation should be coded as psychological or logical. These indeterminate examples were all assigned to the psychological category. There were no clear examples of psychologising in the Game with Rules experiment.

Therefore, the results of these three experiments do not provide evidence of a strong tendency to psychologise. Rather, the results indicate that the children usually did give explanations which were appropriate (at least in general terms) to the phenomenon they were asked to explain.

3.5 Discussion

These elicited production studies give a promising picture of the young child's ability to give well-formed and appropriate explanations. As in Hood's and McCabe and Peterson's studies of spontaneous speech, there were very few cause-effect inversions. The present studies extend the previous findings by showing that the low inversion rate occurs not only when children are explaining psychological phenomena, but also when they are explaining physical or logical phenomena. Furthermore, the children demonstrated an ability to vary the type of relation which they expressed to take account of the type of phenomenon. In particular, they did not tend to psychologise. This picture of the child's ability stands in sharp contrast to the picture presented by Piaget's work and by the comprehension experiments which were reviewed in the previous chapter.

The finding that the inversion rate was not affected by the type of phenomenon demonstrates the importance of drawing a distinction between what children *can* talk about and what they usually *do* talk about. Although young children may tend to talk mostly about psychological relations, they can be encouraged to talk about physical and logical relations.

In this study, the physical and logical phenomena were presented in the context of motives and purposes. For example, in the Ker Plunk experiment, the child was told that the experimenter did not want the marbles to fall down and make a loud noise. Similarly, in the Game with Rules experiment, the arbitrary rules were presented in the context of a purpose which the child could readily appreciate: the purpose of winning the game. In other words, these tasks were what Donaldson (1978) terms 'embedded tasks'. It is possible that if less embedded tasks were used, the children would have more difficulty with the physical and logical phenomena than with the psychological phenomena.

Another feature of the present study is that it made use of phenomena with which young children would probably be familiar. For instance, although most of the children had not actually encountered the Ker Plunk toy before, the physical events which were made to occur in the Ker Plunk experiment (e.g. removing support, falling) were presumably familiar. Keil's findings (1979) indicate that even $1\frac{1}{2}$-year-olds regard the removal of support as a plausible cause for an object falling. It seems likely that children's performance would be poorer for unfamiliar than for familiar phenomena. This has implications for the interpretation both of the finding that the inversion rate was not affected by the type of phenomenon and of the finding that the children did not tend to psychologise.

If, on the whole, children are less familiar with physical and logical phenomena than with psychological phenomena, then they may tend to produce more inversions when they are explaining non-psychological phenomena than when they are explaining psychological phenomena. For this reason, a certain amount of caution is required when interpreting the present finding that the type of phenomenon did not affect the inversion rate. This finding indicates that the type of phenomenon does not always have an effect on the well-formedness of the child's utterances, but not necessarily that the type of phenomenon never affects the level of performance. On the other hand, it is worth noting that apparent content effects may actually be familiarity effects in disguise. It would be interesting to investigate the effect of the familiarity of the phenomenon (and of the 'embeddedness' of the task) on the children's ability to produce non-inverted causal utterances in each of the three content categories. However, this was not done in the present study, since it would have conflicted with the general aim of providing natural contexts for the elicitation of explanations and causal expressions.

Discussion

The finding that the children did not show a strong tendency to psychologise may also be partly attributable to the familiarity of the phenomena. Studies of children's understanding of physical causality (Huang, 1943; Berzonsky, 1971) have shown that children tend to psychologise when they are asked to explain an unfamiliar phenomenon or when the phenomenon cannot readily be explained in physical terms. On the other hand, the same children will give physical explanations when the phenomenon is more familiar or when a demonstration of the phenomenon provides them with a means of constructing a reasonable physical explanation. These results, together with the results of the present studies, suggest that psychologising is something which children turn to only as a last resort. In more favourable circumstances, young children do reveal an ability to match the type of explanation to the type of phenomenon. They do show some understanding of what constitutes a plausible explanation for a given phenomenon. In the next chapter, it will be argued that this understanding underlies children's ability to produce and comprehend causal sentences appropriately.

4   The empirical mode

4.1 Introduction

4.1.1 *A puzzling discrepancy*

The results of the elicited production studies, together with those of Hood's and McCabe and Peterson's studies, indicate that children understand the directional element of the causal connectives' meaning well before the age of 5. On the other hand, the results of most of the comprehension experiments reported in the literature seem to suggest that the directional element is not understood until the age of about 7 or 8. This discrepancy calls for an explanation. The experiment which will be reported in this chapter was designed to test one hypothesis about what the explanation might be.

Most of the previous comprehension experiments have been based on the assumption that answering the question:

'At what age do children understand the directional element of *because* and *so?*'

is equivalent to answering the question:

'At what age do children know that *because* is followed by a reference to the event which happened first, whereas *so* is followed by a reference to the event which happened next?'

In this chapter, I shall challenge the assumption that these two questions are equivalent, and I shall put forward the hypothesis that the child's understanding of the directional element is initially based on causal direction rather than temporal order. (See section 4.1.4.) In order to assess children's knowledge of the causal connectives' role as indicators of causal direction, it will be necessary to consider a third question:

'At what age do children know that *because* is followed by a reference to the cause, whereas *so* is followed by a reference to the effect?'

4.1.2 *Linguistic analysis of sentences in the empirical mode* (See section 1.5.)

Since most of the previous experiments have been based on the empirical mode, the present experiment was also based on the empirical mode. In the empirical mode, an event/state, Y, is explained in terms of a temporally prior event/state, X, which is a physical or psychological cause of Y. Sentences having one of the following forms are acceptable:

(4.1) *Y because X.*
(4.2) *X so Y.*
(4.3) *Because X, Y,*

while sentences having one of the following forms are unacceptable:

(4.4) **X because Y.*
(4.5) **Y so X.*
(4.6) **Because Y, X.*

Thus, the meaning of *because* and *so* includes a directional element which can be captured by saying that *because* must be followed by X, whereas *so* must be followed by Y. Since X is both the cause of Y and temporally prior to Y, the directional element could, in principle, be described either in terms of causal direction or in terms of temporal order. In other words, we could say either that *because* is followed by a reference to the cause or that *because* is followed by a reference to the first event. However, the causal direction description is more powerful in that it also allows us to capture the distinction between causal and temporal connectives. For example, we could say that *because* is followed by a reference to the cause, and that *after* is followed by a reference to the first event. Rules of implication could then be used to take account of the interdependence of causal direction and temporal order. In this analysis, causal direction is more basic than temporal order as far as the meaning of the causal connectives is concerned.

Although the sentences *Y because X*, *X so Y* and *Because X, Y* are all equivalent in their truth-conditions, they differ from one another in other respects. For the *so* sentence and the *because*-initial sentence, the order-of-mention coincides with the order-of-occurrence of the events, whereas for the *because*-medial sentence these two orders do not coincide. However, *because*-initial sentences are relatively rare in spoken discourse. Therefore, for most of the sentences which young children encounter, the order-of-mention coincides with the order-of-occurrence for *so* sentences but not for *because* sentences.

The sentences *Y because X* and *X so Y* also differ with respect to their thematic structure. Linguists frequently draw a distinction between the theme and the rheme. The theme is the expression which the speaker uses to identify what she is talking about, and the rheme is the expression which contains the information which the speaker wishes to communicate (Lyons, 1977). In English sentences, the theme usually precedes the rheme. Traditionally, the theme–rheme distinction has been applied to phrases within a simple sentence. However, the scope of the distinction can be extended to apply to clauses within a complex sentence. In this way, the thematic structure of *because* and *so* sentences could be analysed as:

THEME   RHEME

(4.7) *The window broke because a ball hit it.*

THEME   RHEME

(4.8) *A ball hit the window so the window broke.*

In (4.7), the theme corresponds to the expression which is used to state what is being explained, and the rheme corresponds to the explanation. In (4.8), this pattern is reversed: the clause which provides the explanation comes first. This difference in thematic structure is related to a difference in the functions which the utterances corresponding to (4.7) and (4.8) are likely to serve. If the speaker's aim is to explain the event referred to by *the window broke*, then she will probably make *the window broke* the theme and produce an utterance corresponding to (4.7). If, on the other hand, her aim is to describe a sequence of events, then she will probably make the first event the theme so that the order-of-mention reflects the chronological order of the events. Therefore, she will produce an utterance corresponding to (4.8). Although this utterance will contain information about causal direction, the speaker's primary aim is not to express a causal relation, but to describe what happened.

Thus, it can be argued that while the natural order for a description is 'first event – second event', the natural order for an explanation is 'what is being explained – explanation' and therefore 'second event – first event'. It may be that *Y because X* sentences constitute a more powerful means of expressing causal relations than *X so Y* sentences do, precisely because of the mismatch between the order-of-mention and the order-of-occurrence in *because* sentences. If the unmarked clause order is the one which corresponds to the chronological order of the events, then, when a hearer encounters the opposite clause order, she is likely to assume that the speaker had a special reason for choosing the marked version and to ask herself what that reason might be. In this way, the use of a *Y because X* sentence may draw the hearer's attention to the fact that the speaker intends to express a causal relation. This, in turn, will make the causal link more salient in the *because* sentence than in the corresponding *so* sentence.

Clark (1973), in discussing temporal conjunctions such as *before* and *after*, puts forward an argument similar to the one advanced here. She argues that the alternative constructions for describing time sequences serve different functions, and that the thematic structure plays an important role in determining which construction is used.

4.1.3 *A temporal order task*

To illustrate the basis of the predictions for the present experiment, we shall now look more closely at Emerson's (1979) picture-sequence task. However, the arguments advanced in this chapter apply to temporal order tasks in general, rather than to Emerson's task alone.

In Emerson's picture-sequence task (PST), the child was presented with two static picture-strips, each depicting a sequence of events. The two picture-strips differed only with respect to the order of the events. After describing each picture-strip, the experimenter read out a sentence which referred to the events in the pictures, and asked the child to choose the picture-strip which 'goes with the sentence'.

All the sentences used in this experiment contained *because*. Half of the sentences had the form *Y because X* and half had the form *Because X, Y*. If the children were using an order-of-mention strategy, then their responses would be correct for the *because*-initial items but incorrect for the *because*-medial items.

Emerson also included a comparison between reversible and non-reversible sentences. For non-reversible sentences, one event-order is plausible and the other is implausible, whereas, for reversible sentences, the two event-orders are equally plausible. On the basis of an analogy with research on children's comprehension of the passive (e.g. Bever, 1970), Emerson argues that children may make use of the semantic cues to event-order which are provided by the content of the non-reversible sentences. This would enable the children to give correct responses to non-reversible items even if they did not understand the meaning of the connective. On the other hand, for reversible sentences, the connective is the only cue to event-order, so the children would not be able to give consistently correct responses to reversible items unless they understood the meaning of the connective. Therefore, Emerson predicted that performance would be better on non-reversible items than on reversible items.

Emerson found that performance was significantly better for *because*-initial sentences than for *because*-medial sentences, and she interprets this as evidence that the children were using an order-of-mention strategy. Although performance was better for non-reversible sentences than for reversible sentences, the difference was not statistically significant. (It was significant in Emerson's other task, the first/last task.)

Emerson argues that the best estimate of the age at which children understand *because* is obtained by considering only their performance on the reversible *because*-medial items, since the children cannot succeed on these items by relying on an order-of-mention strategy or semantic probability cues. She found that the children in the youngest age group (5;8 to 6;7) did not give reliably correct responses to these critical items, but that the children in the 7;6 to 8;6 group did. Therefore, the results indicate that until the age of about $7\frac{1}{2}$ years, children lack the knowledge that the event which is referred to immediately after *because* actually occurred first. However, Emerson does not restrict herself to drawing conclusions about the child's knowledge of the temporal order element. She also claims that:

After about age 5, the development of *because* appears to be the development of some…meaning component that we might call ORDER (X, Y), that assigns X, the cause or first-occurring event, to the clause immediately following *because* in the sentence, and assigns Y, the effect and second-occurring event, to the other event named in the remaining clause. The child does not appear to attach this meaning component ORDER (X, Y) to *because* until about age 7 or 8. (p. 300).

On the basis of a task designed to assess understanding of the temporal order element of *because*, Emerson draws a conclusion which applies not only to temporal order but also to causal direction. It is the validity of this more general conclusion which is at issue. There are two main reasons for challenging this conclusion. First, the way in which it has been arrived at is invalid. Second, the results of the elicited production studies indicate that preschool children do understand the directional element of the meaning of *because*.

4.1.4 *The causal direction hypothesis*

In section 4.1.2 we saw that the causal connectives can convey information about both causal direction and temporal order. These two types of information can be summarised as follows:

(a) Information about causal direction:
   Because introduces a cause.
   So introduces an effect.
(b) Information about temporal order:
   Because introduces the event which happened first.
   So introduces the event which happened next.

The causal connectives' primary function is to convey information about causal direction. Their function of conveying information about temporal order is a secondary function which is derived from the primary function via our knowledge about the nature of causality. For example, given the knowledge that *because* introduces a cause and that causes generally precede their effects, it is possible to infer that the event mentioned after *because* happened before the event mentioned in the other clause of the sentence.

Introduction

The main hypothesis tested by the experiment reported in this chapter is that:

The child's knowledge of the directional element of the causal connectives' meaning is initially based on the connectives' primary function of indicating causal direction. Knowledge of the causal connectives' secondary function of indicating temporal order develops later.

This hypothesis will be referred to as the 'causal direction' hypothesis. It predicts that children will perform better on a task which allows them to make use of knowledge about causal direction than on a task which requires knowledge about temporal order. Therefore, the present experiment (Experiment 4) was designed to compare performance on these two types of task: the causal task and the temporal task.

The proposal that the child may know that *because* is followed by a reference to the cause and yet not know that *because* is followed by a reference to the first event may seem rather paradoxical. Given that a cause precedes its effect (within the context of the empirical mode), it follows that if *because* introduces the cause, then *because* must also introduce the first event. However, this does not necessarily mean that *knowing* that *because* introduces the cause is equivalent to *knowing* that it introduces the first event. For example, the child might know that *because* introduces the cause and that causes precede their effects, and yet fail to make the inference which would yield the conclusion that *because* introduces the first event. Research into children's understanding of causality (see section 2.2.2) indicates that young children have a complex concept of 'plausible cause' which includes much more than just the knowledge that causes precede their effects. Furthermore, there is some evidence to suggest that knowledge about temporal order may not be the most salient aspect of young children's 'plausible cause' concept (Sophian and Huber, 1984).

4.1.5 *Other predictions*

The items used in Experiment 4 varied in terms of content and reversibility. Previous studies would lead one to predict that performance would be better for sentences with psychological content than for sentences with physical content, and that performance would be better for non-reversible sentences than for reversible sentences.

Also, performance on *Y because X* sentences was compared with performance on *X so Y* sentences. (This was considered preferable to comparing performance on *because*-medial sentences with performance on *because*-initial sentences, since the children would probably be very unfamiliar with the *because*-initial sentences.) Previous studies using temporal order tasks had found that the children tended to adopt an order-of-mention strategy. Therefore, it was predicted that in the temporal task performance would be better for *so* sentences than for *because* sentences, since the order-of-mention coincides with the order-of-occurrence for *so* sentences but not for *because* sentences. On the other hand, if, in the causal task, the child's performance is guided by knowledge of the causal direction element of the connectives' meaning, then she would not find *so* sentences easier than *because* sentences. Indeed, it could be argued that she would find *because* sentences easier since they are consistent with the natural order for giving an explanation. (See section 4.1.2.) Therefore, it was predicted that in the causal task performance on *because* sentences would be either equal to or better than performance on *so* sentences.

4.2 Method for Experiment 4

4.2.1 *Subjects*

There were 32 subjects in each of three age groups: 4;11 to 5;11 (mean = 5;4), 8;0 to 8;11 (mean = 8;6), and 10;3 to 11;2 (mean = 10;9). The two younger groups each consisted of 18 boys and 14 girls, and the oldest group consisted of 12 boys and 20 girls. All the children were attending the same local authority primary school (Granton Primary, Edinburgh). An adult control group consisting of 12 psychology undergraduates was also included.

4.2.2 *Design*

There were two between-subjects variables: age (5 years/8 years/10 years/adult) and type of task (causal/temporal). Within each age group, half of the subjects received the causal task and half received the temporal task. The causal and temporal groups were matched for mean age, and, as far as possible, for age range.

There were also three within-subjects variables, each with two levels: content (physical/psychological), reversibility (reversible/non-reversible) and connective (*because*/*so*). The content and reversibility variables yield four categories of causal sequence:

    (i) physical reversible
   (ii) physical non-reversible
  (iii) psychological reversible
  (iv) psychological non-reversible.

Two examples of each category of sequence were constructed, and then each causal sequence was used to construct one *because* item and one *so* item, giving a total of 16 items. (See Appendix 2.) This set was divided into two parallel subsets, each containing eight items, one for each causal sequence. For each of the four categories of sequence there was one *because* sentence and one *so* sentence in each subset. The sequences which were paired with *because* sentences in one subset were paired with *so* sentences in the other subset. All the subjects received both subsets, but in two separate sessions. The order of presentation of the subsets was counter-balanced within each group of subjects. The order of presentation of the causal sequences was constant both across subjects and between sessions. This fixed order was constructed in such a way that the effects of certain response strategies (such as alternating between the top and bottom pictures) would be evenly distributed across the various types of item. The same set of eight causal sequences was used as the basis for the items in both the causal task and the temporal task.

Most previous experiments have been based on causal sequences consisting of only two events. However, this makes it difficult to construct a task which does not require the child to demonstrate knowledge of the temporal order element of the connectives' meaning. In the present experiment, each item was based on a causal sequence which consisted of three events: $A \rightarrow B \rightarrow C$. All the stimulus sentences began with a reference to event B. In the causal condition, the child's task was to complete a sentence fragment which had one of the following forms:

(4.9) *B because...*
(4.10) *B so...*

Therefore, the child was being asked to choose between the cause (A) and the effect (C) of a given event. The temporal task was based on Emerson's picture-sequence task. The child was presented with a sentence which had one of the following forms:

(4.11) *B because A*
(4.12) *B so C*

The child's task was to select a picture-strip to match the sentence. For *because* sentences, the child had to choose between a picture-strip depicting event A followed by event B ($A \rightarrow B$), and one depicting event B followed by event A ($B \rightarrow A$). For *so* sentences, she had to choose between $B \rightarrow C$ and $C \rightarrow B$. Therefore, in the temporal task, the two alternative responses differed with respect to the order in which the events were depicted, whereas, in the causal task, the two alternative responses differed with respect to the semantic content of the clauses. The temporal task required a choice between two different event-orders, while the causal task required a choice between two different events.

4.2.3 *Materials*

For each task, the materials consisted of: a set of video-taped causal sequences, a set of black-and-white line drawings, and a set of sentences (or sentence fragments).

The causal sequences were acted out using two hand-puppets (Coco and
(Daisy), and were recorded on black-and-white video-tape. (One of the
sequences also involved two dolls, John and Mary.) Each sequence was acted
out in two orders: A → B → C and C → B → A.[1] The video-tape was edited to
produce two sets of video-taped sequences: one for the causal task and one
for the temporal task. In the causal set, each sequence was shown only in
its standard order (A → B → C), and each sequence occurred twice in succession. In the temporal set, each sequence occurred twice in succession:
once in its standard order (A → B → C) and once in its reversed order
(C → B → A). The order of presentation of the standard and reversed orders
was counter-balanced across sequences. At the beginning of both sets, there
were two sequences of events which were not causally related. These were
used as a basis for practice items.

For each task, a set of black-and-white line drawings was constructed.
Corresponding to each sequence in the causal task, there were two picture-
cards: one depicting event A and the other depicting event C. For each
sequence in the temporal task, the picture-cards were stuck together in pairs
to yield four picture-strips depicting the event sequences: A → B, B → A, B → C
and C → B.

Corresponding to each sequence in the causal task, there were two sentence
fragments, one of the form *B because*...(e.g. *Daisy hits Coco because*...) and
one of the form *B so*...(e.g. *Daisy hits Coco so*...). For each sequence in the
temporal task, there were two sentences, one of the form *B because A* (e.g.
Daisy hits Coco because he pulls her hair) and one of the form *B so C* (e.g. *Daisy
hits Coco so he pushes her*).

4.2.4 *Procedure*

Each child was tested individually in an empty classroom. The child and
experimenter sat side by side in front of some portable video equipment. At
the beginning of the first session the child was shown drawings of the two
puppets, Coco and Daisy. Then the child was asked to 'watch the television',
and she saw a short section of video-tape in which the puppets introduced
themselves.

For each item in the causal task, the sequence was presented on the
video-screen. Then the experimenter read out the incomplete sentence, and
placed the two picture-cards on the table in front of the child. The pictures

were arranged vertically on the table, and the position of the correct picture was counter-balanced across items. The child was asked to describe each picture ('What's happening in this picture?'), and the experimenter expanded on or corrected these descriptions where necessary. Next, the experimenter said, 'I want you to watch the television and then give me the picture that makes the story right.' The child was shown the sequence again, and the experimenter repeated the incomplete sentence. Usually, the child completed the sentence without prompting, and picked up the corresponding picture. If she did not do so, she was asked to 'choose the picture that will make the story right...And tell me about it.' Finally, the experimenter tried to elicit the whole sentence from the child ('Now, can you say it all by yourself?'). If necessary, the experimenter prompted the child with the first few words of the sentence. In the first session, the child received two practice items before the eight test items. These practice items were used to train the child on the sentence completion and picture selection procedures. They involved completing sentence fragments which ended with *and*.

For each item in the temporal task, the experimenter placed one of the picture-strips on the table in front of the child, and asked the child to describe it. Once the strip had been correctly described, the experimenter said, 'Now let's see it on the television,' and the sequence corresponding to the strip was shown. Then the experimenter removed the picture-strip and replaced it with the strip depicting the opposite event-order. After this strip had been correctly described, the corresponding video-taped sequence was presented. Finally, the experimenter placed both picture-strips on the table (one above the other), read out the sentence twice in succession, and asked the child, 'Which strip of pictures goes with what I said?' The position of the correct picture-strip and the order of presentation of the two versions of the sequences were counter-balanced across items. At the beginning of the first session, the child received two practice items. One of the sentences consisted of two clauses linked by *and then*, and the other sentence consisted of two clauses linked by *but first*. These items were used to train the child to select the strip which corresponded to the order-of-occurrence of the events rather than the strip which corresponded to the order-of-mention. It was hoped that this would reduce the ambiguity of the phrase 'goes with'.

Table 10 summarises the procedures used in each task. The same procedures were used with the adult subjects, except that they were tested in groups, wrote down their responses, and received both subsets of items in a single session.

The procedure used in the temporal task differs from that used in Emerson's PST in four main ways. First, Emerson did not include any training items for the PST. Second, my temporal task is based on causal sequences consisting of three, rather than two, events. However, for any given item, the subjects

Table 10. *Summary of procedures for Experiment 4*

	'Because' items	'So' items
Casual task		
1. Video-taped sequence	A → B → C	A → B → C
2. E reads sentence fragment	B because...	B so...
3. E presents picture-cards	A and C	A and C
4. S describes picture-cards		
5. Video-taped sequence	A → B → C	A → B → C
6. E repeats sentence fragment	B because...	B so...
7. S chooses picture-card	A or C	A or C
8. S completes sentence		
9. S says whole sentence		
Temporal task		
1. E presents one picture-strip	A → B or B → A	B → C or C → B
2. S describes picture-strip		
3. Video-taped sequence corresponding to picture-strip	A → B → C or C → B → A	A → B → C or C → B → A
4. E presents second picture-strip	opposite order to (1)	opposite order to (1)
5. S describes second picture-strip		
6. Video-taped sequence corresponding to second picture-strip	opposite order to (3)	opposite order to (3)
7. E presents both picture-strips	A → B and B → A	B → C and C → B
8. E reads sentence twice	B because A	B so C
9. S chooses picture-strip to match sentence		

had to deal with only two of the events from the three-event sequence. Although the video-taped sequence showed all three events, each sentence and each pair of picture-strips represented only two of these events. Third, the present experiment used *because* and *so* sentences, while Emerson's experiment used two types of *because* sentence. Fourth, my experiment made use of video-taped sequences, whereas Emerson's did not.

The main reason for using video-taped sequences was that it seemed likely that the causal relations could be encoded more powerfully in a dynamic representation than in a static representation. In particular, the continuity of causal sequences can be preserved when video-taped sequences are used. In the causal task, the video-taped sequences play a particularly important role. Unless the subjects are given some contextual information, both of the potential responses to the reversible items would have to be regarded as equally correct. This contextual information is provided by the video-taped sequences. In the temporal task, all the information which is required in order to make the correct response is contained in the sentence, so the video-taped sequences play a less crucial role than in the causal task. Nevertheless, the video-tapes were used in the temporal task so that it would be as similar as

Table 11. *Number of subjects passing each task*[a]

	Causal task	Temporal task	
5 years	7	0	$p < 0.01$
8 years	14	2	$p < 0.001$
10 years	15	5	$p < 0.001$
Adults	6	6	NS

[a] i.e. scoring at least 12 out of 16.
The maximum possible per cell is 6 for the adults and 16 for all the other age groups. The significance levels are based on chi-square or Fisher's exact probability tests.

possible to the causal task. For the non-reversible items in the temporal task, the reversed video-taped sequences were, of course, rather bizarre. However, if the subjects had been shown only the normal sequences, they could simply have selected the picture-strip which matched the video-taped sequence without considering the sentence at all.

4.2.5 *Scoring*

Each subject was given one point for each item which she responded to correctly. In the causal task, the scoring was based on the choice of picture and the sentence completion, rather than on the subject's production of the complete sentence.

4.3 **Results**

4.3.1 *The causal direction hypothesis*

The causal direction hypothesis predicts that performance will be better on the causal task than on the temporal task. Table 11 shows the number of subjects who passed each task. In order to pass, a subject had to give the correct response to at least 12 out of the 16 items. (From the binomial distribution, the probability of this outcome occurring by chance is less than 0.05.) The significance of the differences between the two tasks was then tested using a chi-square test. The results indicate that performance was significantly better on the causal task than on the temporal task, for all age groups except the adults, who were performing at ceiling level on both tasks. As Table 12 shows, a similar pattern of results is obtained when the comparison is based on the mean number of correct responses for each group.

The absolute level of performance in the causal task is also noteworthy. Almost half of the 5-year-olds and almost all the older children passed the causal task. Similarly, the mean score for all the age groups is considerably

Table 12. *Mean number of correct responses for each group*

	Causal task	Temporal task	
5 years	12.12	7.38	$p < 0.001$
8 years	13.12	8.19	$p < 0.001$
10 years	14.81	10.94	$p < 0.01$
Adults	16.00	16.00	NS

The maximum possible per cell is 16. The significance levels are based on 1-tailed Mann-Whitney U tests.

Table 13. *Comparison of causal and temporal tasks: mean number of correct responses to 'because' items*

	Causal task	Temporal task	
5 years	6.69	3.50	$p < 0.001$
8 years	7.75	1.69	$p < 0.001$
10 years	7.75	2.94	$p < 0.001$

The significance levels are obtained from Mann-Whitney U tests (1-tailed). Maximum possible per cell = 8.

Table 14. *Comparison of causal and temporal tasks: mean number of correct responses to 'so' items*

	Causal task	Temporal task	
5 years	5.44	3.88	$p < 0.05$
8 years	5.38	6.50	$p < 0.025^*$
10 years	7.06	8.00	$p < 0.01^*$

The significance levels are obtained from Mann-Whitney U tests (1-tailed). An asterisk indicates that the difference is in the opposite direction from that predicted by the causal direction hypothesis. Maximum possible per cell = 8.

higher than the score (of 8) which one would expect if the children were simply responding at chance level. These findings imply that even 5-year-olds have some knowledge of the directional element of the connectives' meaning.

Tables 13 and 14 compare performance on the causal task with performance on the temporal task for each of the connectives. The causal direction hypothesis receives support from the results for the *because* items and from the results for the 5-year-olds' performance on the *so* items. On the other hand, the 8- and 10-year-olds' performance on the *so* items was better in the temporal task than in the causal task. However, the high level of performance

Table 15. *Comparison of mean scores on 'because' and 'so' in temporal task*

	Because	So	
5 years	3.50	3.88	NS
8 years	1.69	6.50	$p < 0.005$
10 years	2.94	8.00	$p < 0.005$

The significance levels are obtained from Wilcoxon's matched-pairs signed-ranks tests (1-tailed). Maximum possible per cell = 8.

Table 16. *Number of subjects assigned to order-of-mention strategy[a]*

	Temporal task	Causal task
5 years	5	1
8 years	10	0
10 years	11	0

[a] Subjects whose responses were consistent with order-of-mention strategy for at least 12 out of the 16 items.

for *so* items in the temporal task is probably an artefact of the subjects' use of an order-of-mention strategy. (See section 4.3.2.)

4.3.2 *'Because' and 'so'*

It was predicted that, in the temporal task, the children would adopt an order-of-mention strategy, and so would perform better on *so* items than on *because* items. As Table 15 shows, the results for the 8-year-olds and 10-year-olds confirm this prediction. A more direct test of the hypothesis that the children were following an order-of-mention strategy was carried out by examining the response profiles of the individual subjects. A subject was judged to have been following the order-of-mention strategy if at least 12 (out of 16) of her responses were consistent with that strategy. As Table 16 shows, more than half of the 8- and 10-year-olds were assigned to the order-of-mention strategy for the temporal task. In contrast, none of the 8- or 10-year-olds who received the causal task could be assigned to the order-of-mention strategy. This indicates that the order-of-mention strategy is a task-specific strategy.

It was predicted that, in the causal task, performance on *because* items would be equal to or better than performance on *so* items. The results presented in Table 17 indicate that the children did indeed perform better on *because* than on *so*. Further evidence that children can deal with *because* sentences better

Table 17. *Comparison of mean scores on 'because' and 'so' in causal task*

	Because	So	
5 years	6.69	5.44	$p < 0.05$
8 years	7.75	5.38	$p < 0.005$
10 years	7.75	7.06	$p < 0.05$

The significance levels are obtained from Wilcoxon's matched-pairs signed-ranks tests (1-tailed). Maximum possible per cell = 8.

Table 18. *Mean number of connective changes of each type in causal task[a]*

	Because → So	So → Because	
5 years	0.50	2.64	$p < 0.01$
8 years	0.86	1.64	NS
10 years	0.12	0.56	NS

[a] The data used in constructing this table do not include the data from two of the 5-year-olds and two of the 8-year-olds, because some responses to this part of the task were lost due to recording faults.
The significance levels are obtained from Wilcoxon matched-pairs signed-ranks tests (2-tailed). Maximum possible per cell = 8.

than *so* sentences comes from the results of asking the children to produce the whole sentence after they had completed each sentence fragment. Sometimes, when the children tried to say the whole sentence, they changed the connective which had been present in the original sentence fragment. In these cases, *so* was replaced by *because* more frequently than *because* was replaced by *so*. (See Table 18). This suggests that the children had a preference for producing *because* sentences rather than *so* sentences.

4.3.3 *Age comparisons*

A Kruskal-Wallis one-way analysis of variance revealed that there were significant age effects both in the causal task ($p < 0.001$) and in the temporal task ($p < 0.01$). Mann-Whitney U tests (2-tailed) indicated that the 10-year-olds performed significantly better than the 8-year-olds ($p < 0.02$ for the causal task and $p < 0.05$ for the temporal task), but that the differences between the 8-year-olds and the 5-year-olds were not significant.

Further Kruskal-Wallis ANOVAs were carried out to test the effect of age for each connective separately. Significant age effects were obtained for the *because* items in the causal task ($p < 0.01$), for the *so* items in the causal task ($p < 0.01$), and for the *so* items in the temporal task ($p < 0.001$), but not for

Table 19. *Comparison of physical and psychological items with respect to mean number of correct responses*[a]

	Physical	Psychological	
Causal task			
5 years	5.94	6.19	NS
8 years	6.31	6.81	NS
10 years	7.44	7.38	NS
Temporal task			
5 years	3.50	3.88	NS
8 years	4.12	4.06	NS
10 years	5.31	5.62	NS

[a] Wilcoxon matched-pairs signed-ranks tests, 1-tailed.

the *because* items in the temporal task. In the causal task, the 8-year-olds performed significantly better than the 5-year-olds on *because* items, and the 10-year-olds performed significantly better than the 8-year-olds on *so* items. In the temporal task, significant improvements in performance on *so* items occurred both between 5 and 8 years and between 8 and 10 years. These increases are partly attributable to an increase with age in the number of subjects using an order-of-mention strategy. (See Table 16.) Some of the younger subjects either did not appear to be following any consistent strategy or used other strategies such as always selecting the lower picture.

4.3.4 *Content and reversibility*

As Table 19 shows, the results failed to confirm the prediction that performance would be better for psychological items than for physical items.

It was predicted that performance would be better for non-reversible items than for reversible items. The results presented in Table 20 show that in the causal task there was a significant effect in the predicted direction for the 8-year-olds and the 10-year-olds. However, none of the other differences was significant.

4.4 **Discussion**

The results of the physical/psychological comparison do not lend any support to Piaget's claim that relations of psychological causality are understood before relations of physical causality. On the other hand, they are totally consistent with the results of the elicited production studies. (See Chapter 3.) Therefore, we can reject the strong claim that young children cannot express and understand relations of physical causality adequately. However, we

Table 20. *Comparison of reversible and non-reversible items with respect to mean number of correct responses*[a]

	Reversible	Non-reversible	
Causal task			
5 years	5.88	6.25	NS
8 years	6.25	6.88	$p < 0.05$
10 years	7.06	7.75	$p < 0.01$
Temporal task			
5 years	3.94	3.44	NS
8 years	4.25	3.94	NS
10 years	5.62	5.31	NS

[a] Wilcoxon matched-pairs signed-ranks tests, 1-tailed.

cannot reject the weaker claim that young children's ability to express and understand relations of psychological causality exceeds their ability to express and understand relations of physical causality, since my studies were deliberately designed to include only phenomena with which the child would probably be familiar.

The results for the temporal task fail to support the hypothesis that non-reversible sentences are easier than reversible sentences. This is consistent with the results of Emerson's PST. In her first/last task (FLT), Emerson did find a reversibility effect. Emerson explains the lack of a reversibility effect in the PST by arguing that the children may be better able to deal with reversible sentences when the two alternative sequences are presented to them (as in the PST) than when they have to create the alternatives for themselves (as in the FLT). However, this explanation is not applicable to the present findings. With the possible exception of the 10-year-old group, it was not the case that the children were managing to deal with the reversible sentences as well as with the non-reversible sentences, but rather that they were failing to deal with either type of sentence adequately. An inspection of the response profiles of the individual subjects reveals that, even in the oldest age group, none of the subjects performed markedly better on the non-reversible items than on the reversible items. In the oldest age group, all the children could either be categorised as following the order-of-mention strategy or as passing the task. A similar, although less consistent, pattern can be observed for the 8-year-old group. This suggests that the most serious problem which the children faced in dealing with the temporal task was that of resisting the order-of-mention strategy. It may be that the tendency to follow an order-of-mention strategy was so strong that it masked any tendency to make use of semantic plausibility.

It might be argued that the lack of a reversibility effect is attributable to the particular sentences which were used in the present study. However, the fact that there was a significant reversibility effect for two of the age groups in the causal task argues against such an explanation.

The findings for the causal task support Emerson's hypothesis that non-reversible sentences are easier than reversible sentences. However, they do not support her claim that using performance on non-reversible sentences to assess the child's knowledge of the connectives' meaning leads to an over-estimation of the child's ability. Such a claim would be valid in relation to the temporal task, but not in relation to the causal task. In the causal condition, the children's task is to choose between a cause and an effect, and the only clue as to which they should choose for a given item is provided by the connective. Therefore, in order to succeed in the task, the children must take account of the meaning of the connective. It is difficult to conceive of a strategy which could produce correct responses for non-reversible sentences but not for reversible sentences irrespective of the connective used. Therefore, correct responses to non-reversible items in the causal task do imply that the children have some knowledge of the connectives' meaning. The fact that performance was better for non-reversible items than for reversible items suggests that pragmatic cues can help children to demonstrate their knowledge. However, this is not the same as saying that pragmatic cues can help children to pass the task when they lack the relevant semantic knowledge. For tasks like the temporal task, including pragmatic cues may produce false positives. In contrast, for tasks like the causal task, eliminating pragmatic cues may produce false negatives.

In the causal task, the information about which event is the cause and which is the effect is provided by the video-taped sequence. For non-reversible items, this information could be reinforced by the child's knowledge of pragmatic plausibility. If, on the basis of her world knowledge, the child knows that event A is more likely to be the cause than the effect of event B, and if the video-taped sequence depicts the event sequence $A \rightarrow B \rightarrow C$, then the child has two reasons for selecting A as the cause of B. On the other hand, for reversible items, the child has to rely on the information provided by the video-taped sequence. She has only one reason for selecting A as the cause of B. Therefore, it may be easier for the child to decide which event is the cause and which the effect when the item is non-reversible than when it is reversible. However, it is important to note that knowing which event is the cause and which is the effect is a necessary but not a sufficient pre-condition of success in the task.

The causal direction hypothesis is strongly supported by the finding that performance on the causal task was significantly better than performance on the temporal task. Therefore, we can conclude that children have an understanding of the directional element of the causal connectives' meaning which is based on causal direction rather than on temporal order. This would explain why children can use the causal connectives appropriately in their spontaneous speech and in the elicited production studies long before they can pass a comprehension task based on temporal order. In their spontaneous speech and in the elicited production studies, the children can make use of their knowledge about causal direction, whereas, in a temporal order task, they are required to base their responses on the information which the causal connectives can convey about temporal order.

The fact that young children fail temporal order tasks involving the causal connectives does not necessarily mean that they lack an understanding of temporal order or that they do not know that a cause precedes its effect. It may only mean that young children do not know that *the causal connectives* can provide information about temporal order. Therefore, they do not realise that the causal connectives have any relevance for the way they respond in a temporal order task.

Several studies of children's understanding of causal sequences have provided evidence that young children do indeed know that a cause is temporally prior to its effect (Shultz and Mendelson, 1975; Kun, 1978; Bullock and Gelman, 1979). However, there is also evidence which indicates that children's concept of plausible cause is not restricted to knowledge of the temporal precedence principle (see section 2.2.2). Furthermore, in making causal judgements, young children sometimes neglect temporal order cues and rely on more situation-specific cues (Sophian and Huber, 1984). Thus, while young children know that causes typically precede their effects, this knowledge is perhaps not a particularly salient component of their concept of plausible cause. This would help to explain children's failure to exploit temporal order information in experiments designed to test comprehension of the causal connectives.

The claim that young children know that *because* is followed by a reference to a cause whereas *so* is followed by a reference to an effect implies that they have some understanding as to what constitutes a plausible cause for a given effect. Some evidence that young children do have a notion of 'plausible cause' is provided by the finding that the children in the elicited production studies showed a strong tendency to match their explanations to the type of phenomenon. (See Chapter 3.) Similar evidence is provided by some of the studies of children's understanding of causality. (See section 2.2.2.) In the present experiment, the causal task presents the child with a restricted context, and so the need for knowledge about the plausibility of a cause relative to a particular effect is reduced. Nevertheless, the fact that the children performed better on non-reversible items than on reversible items does suggest that they had some knowledge of cause–effect plausibility.

Although the notion of plausibility is closely related to the notion of sentence reversibility, it is important to draw a distinction between these two notions. The notion of plausibility is much more general than the notion of reversibility. To say that a sentence (*B because A*) is reversible with respect to causal direction or event-order is to say that the probability of A → B is approximately equal to the probability of B → A.

In other words, reversibility is a function of the relative plausibilities of *two* opposing orders or directions. In many experimental tasks, the children are being asked to distinguish between these two orders, so it is easy to see how their performance could be influenced by the degree of reversibility. However, when children are producing language spontaneously, their task is not simply to choose between two opposing orders or directions. Instead, they usually have to construct or complete the causal relation for themselves. For instance, when they are answering a *Why?* question, they are given the effect, but have to supply an appropriate cause. In such cases, knowing that A is the cause will not help the child unless she also knows whether a given item requires her to respond by referring to the cause or by referring to the effect. And, in order to know that, she must understand and take account of the meaning of the connective.

The concept of reversibility is a complex one which merits further discussion and analysis. Although I have treated the reversible/non-reversible distinction as a dichotomy (in order to facilitate comparisons with Emerson's study), reversibility is actually a matter of degree rather than being an all-or-nothing phenomenon. In a reversible sequence, the two alternative event-orders have approximately equal probabilities; whereas, in a non-reversible sequence, one event-order is more probable than the other. However, non-reversible sequences vary with respect to the extent of the difference in plausibility between the two event-orders: the more plausible order may be much more plausible than the alternative order, or it may be only slightly more plausible than the alternative order. Tager-Flusberg (1981) has shown that young children's comprehension of active and passive sentences is influenced not only by whether the sentences are reversible or non-reversible but also by the degree of non-reversibility. (This finding applied to normal children but not autistic children.) Future research might profitably explore the extent to which children's comprehension of the causal connectives is affected by variations along the reversible/non-reversible continuum.

A further complexity is that a distinction can be drawn between the reversibility of an event sequence and the reversibility of the sentence which is used in describing the event sequence. For example, a sequence in which a red ball moves and in so doing causes a blue ball to move could be reversed so that the blue ball moves and in so doing causes the red ball to move. However, the following sentence which could be used to describe the original event sequence is non-reversible:

> *The blue ball moved because the red ball pushed it.*

Conversely, a sentence may be reversible by virtue of the fact that both *Y because X* and *X because Y* can be given plausible interpretations even if the sequence X → Y is not itself reversible.

For example, the sentence:

> *Daisy fell because Coco bumped into her*

can be reversed to give:

> *Coco bumped into Daisy because she fell.*

However, it is not possible to take the event sequence described by the first sentence and simply 'run it backwards' to produce the event sequence described by the second sentence. Of course, in some cases, the distinction between sentence reversibility and event reversibility will collapse. In the present experiment, it was sentence reversibility which was manipulated, though as far as possible examples were selected which did not involve too much of a clash between the two types of reversibility.

The finding that, in the causal task, performance was better for *because* items than for *so* items supports the argument that *Y because X* sentences constitute a more powerful means of expressing causal relations than *X so Y* sentences. (See section 4.1.2.) This, in turn, lends further support to the causal direction hypothesis, since it suggests that the child is being influenced by the way in which *because* and *so* function as indicators of causal direction.

At first sight, it may seem that there is no reason for giving more weight to the finding that performance was better on *because* than on *so* in the causal task than to the apparently contradictory finding that performance was better on *so* than on *because* in the temporal task. However, the connective effect in the temporal task can be explained as a by-product of the order-of-mention strategy.

There are two main ways of viewing the order-of-mention strategy. It could be viewed as a description of the way the child deals with the experimental task. Alternatively, it could be viewed as a description of the child's knowledge of the meaning of *because* and *so*. This would be equivalent to saying that the child thought that both *because* and *so* should be followed by a reference to a subsequent event. The fact that the children did not follow the order-of-mention strategy in the causal task argues against this second interpretation. It is important to remember that whereas the temporal task *requires* the children to make use of knowledge about temporal order, the causal task merely *allows* the children to make use of knowledge about causal direction. Therefore, if the childen really believed that *because* was used to introduce a temporally subsequent event, then their responses in the causal task should have reflected this belief. The fact that they did not suggests that the order-of-mention strategy is specific to certain types of experimental task, and therefore that it would be unwise to draw conclusions about the relative difficulty of *because* and *so* on the basis of such tasks.

It might of course be argued that the connective effect in the causal task is also due to the effects of some strategy. However, it is difficult to imagine what such a strategy would be. The most likely candidate would be the strategy of always basing one's response on the first event shown in the video-taped sequence. Although this is a possible strategy, there are several factors which make it unlikely that the children were following it. First, Kun (1978) found that when 4- to 8-year-olds were asked a nonsense question about the middle event in a three-event sequence, there was no evidence of any response bias. When the children were asked a *Why?* question, they showed a strong tendency to select an antecedent event, whereas when they were asked *What happened next?* they showed a strong tendency to select a consequent event. (In Kun's study the children were simply required to point to the appropriate picture. They did not have to give a verbal response.) Second, Clark (1973) found that when young children were describing event sequences they showed a strong tendency to describe the events in their chronological order. The strategy of always basing one's response on the first event would have to counteract this natural tendency to describe events in their natural order. It seems more likely that the children would relinquish this natural order because they knew that *because* must be followed by a cause than because of some low level strategy. Third, the data obtained in the causal task do not offer much support to the hypothesis that the children were following a 'first event' strategy. Such a strategy would result in the subjects scoring 0 for the *so* items and 8 for the *because* items. However, no subject, in any of the age groups, scored less than 3 (out of 8) for the *so* items. Those subjects who did not 'pass' on the *so* items seemed to be responding at random, rather than following a 'first event' strategy.

Therefore, the results of the causal task do indicate that children understand *because* better than *so*. This conclusion is also supported by the finding that, in the causal task, the only significant improvement with age for performance on *because* items occurred between 5 and 8 years, whereas for *so* items it occurred between 8 and 10 years. Moreover, the age effect for the *because* items seems to represent a slight increase in the consistency of the responses, rather than a dramatic increase in understanding, in that all except one of the 5-year-olds were scoring well above chance on the *because* items. On the other hand, for the *so* items, 9 (out of 16) of the 5-year-olds and 8 of the 8-year-olds scored less than 6 (out of 8), compared with only 2 of the 10-year-olds. This suggests that the age effect for *so* does reflect a considerable increase in understanding.

In summary, the results of Experiment 4 indicate that childen understand the directional element of the causal connectives' meaning in terms of causal direction before they understand that the causal connectives can also convey information about temporal order. The results also suggest that children understand the meaning of *because* better than the meaning of *so*. However, in view of the fact that the linguistic structure of *because* and *so* sentences varies according to the mode of explanation, we should be cautious about drawing a definite conclusion regarding the relative difficulty of *because* and *so* until we have also studied the other modes of explanation.

5   The intentional mode

5.1 Introduction

5.1.1 *Explanations in the intentional mode*

Most of the studies on the development of the causal connectives which are reported in the literature have dealt exclusively with the empirical mode. In Chapter 4, we saw that young children are much more competent at dealing with *because* and *so* in the empirical mode than the results of most previous experiments have suggested. We shall now turn to the question of whether young children's ability extends to the intentional mode or whether it is initially restricted to the empirical mode.

In the intentional mode, an action is explained in terms of the agent's aim or intention. The action is viewed as a goal-directed and purposive element of behaviour. Therefore, an intentional explanation includes a reference to an event or state which occurs (or is expected to occur) *after* the action which is being explained. In this sense, intentional explanations are 'forward-looking', whereas empirical explanations are 'backward-looking' (in that they explain an event/state in terms of a temporally prior event/state).

When a speaker gives an intentional explanation, he asserts that a psychological relation holds between the action and the intention. At the same time, he presupposes that the action is likely to achieve the intended result. The relation between the action and the result may be causal, as in:

(5.1) *John wound up the toy car because he wanted it to go.*

In some cases, though, the action does not actually *cause* the event/state which the agent intends to bring about. Instead, the action *enables* the agent to attain his goal by satisfying a certain pre-condition. An example of an intentional explanation which presupposes a conditional rather than a causal relation would be:

(5.2) *Mary took out her crayons because she wanted to do some colouring in.*

The action (of taking out her crayons) enables Mary to satisfy the condition that in order to colour in, it is necessary to have an appropriate instrument.

Both the causal and the conditional relations may be either physical (as in the above examples) or psychological, as in:

(5.3) *John put a mouse in Mary's bed because he wanted to frighten her.*
(Psychological + Causal)
(5.4) *Mary put on a pretty dress because she was going to a party.*
(Psychological + Conditional)

For all four types of intentional explanation, three main components can be identified: the reason for the action, the action, and the (actual or predicted) result of the action.[1] There is a very close relationship between the reason and the result. On the basis of a sequence consisting of an action and its result, it is possible to infer that the reason for the action was the agent's desire to achieve the result. Conversely, if the result has not actually been observed, an intentional explanation of the action will incorporate a prediction about the probable result. Both the inference and the prediction draw on knowledge of the relation between the action and the result. Despite the interdependence of the reason–action relation and the action–result relation, the speaker must maintain a distinction between the two relations when he is producing causal sentences, since the distinction has certain linguistic consequences.

5.1.2 *Linguistic analysis of sentences in intentional mode*

Miller and Johnson-Laird (1976) present an analysis of the relationship between perceived intentions and perceived causes. Their analysis can be adapted to provide a means of representing the main proposition which is expressed in an intentional explanation:

(5.5) CAUSE (INTEND (Agent, Y), X).

In (5.5), CAUSE and INTEND are two-place predicates, X is the action which is being explained and Y is the result of that action. However, this analysis does not actually capture the relation between X and Y. Searle (1981) proposes that an intention may be broken down into a belief component and a desire component. We might combine this proposal with the analysis given in (5.5) by replacing 'INTEND (Agent, Y)' with the conjunction of (5.6) and (5.7):

(5.6) DESIRE (Agent, Y)
(5.7) BELIEVE (Agent, (CAUSE (X,Y))).

This would yield:

(5.8) CAUSE ((DESIRE (Agent, Y) $\wedge$ BELIEVE (Agent, (CAUSE (X, Y)))), X).

The proposition which (5.8) represents could be described informally by saying that an action (X) is caused by the agent's desire to achieve an event/state (Y) combined with the agent's belief that doing X would cause Y to happen or occur. An example of an intentional explanation which makes all the elements of this analysis explicit would be:

(5.9) *John wound up the toy car because he wanted it to go and he believed that winding it up would make it go.*

This analysis clarifies the way in which the intentional mode is parasitic on the empirical mode. An empirical explanation, such as:

(5.10) *The toy car went because John wound it up.*

expresses a proposition of the form:

(5.11) CAUSE (X, Y).

In the corresponding intentional explanation, this proposition functions as the second argument of the BELIEVE predicate. However, if the intentional explanation presupposes a conditional rather than a causal relation, the second argument of the BELIEVE predicate would have to be modified to:

(5.12) ALLOW (X, Y).

Thus, the intentional mode is more obviously dependent on the empirical mode when the underlying relation is causal than when it is conditional.

An intentional explanation need not be as explicit as example (5.9). The following sentences illustrate the main types of construction which can be used in giving intentional explanations:

(5.13) *John wound up the toy car to make it go.*
(5.14) *John wound up the toy car because he wanted it to go.*
(5.15) *Mary took out her crayons because she was going to do some colouring in.*
(5.16) *John wanted the toy car to go so he wound it up.*
(5.17) *Mary was going to do some colouring in so she took out her crayons.*
(5.18) *John wound up the toy car so (that) it would go.*
(5.19) *Mary took out her crayons so (that) she could do some colouring in.*

In all these types of sentence, the verb which is used to refer to the result of the action (*go*/*do*) occurs in its non-finite form. This non-finite form may either be part of an infinitive construction (as in (5.13)), or part of a modal construction (as in (5.18) and (5.19)), or part of a phrase which refers to the agent's desire or aim (as in (5.14) to (5.17)). All of these patterns contrast with the types of construction which can be used to give an empirical explanation:

(5.20) *The toy car went because John wound it up.*
(5.21) *John wound up the toy car so it went.*

In the empirical mode, a finite verb form (*went*) is used to refer to the result of the action. Empirical sentences are used to express the relation between an action and the result of the action, whereas intentional sentences are used to express the relation between an action and the reason for the action (when the reason corresponds to the agent's intention to achieve a particular result). The distinction between these two type of relation is marked linguistically in the way just outlined. The linguistic distinction is illustrated by the unacceptability of sentences such as:

(5.22) *John wound up the toy car because it went.*

In the empirical mode, *because* is used to introduce a cause, whereas *so* is used to introduce an effect. A similar distinction between *because* and *so* holds in the intentional mode. In (5.14) and (5.15), *because* is followed by a reference to an intention which could be regarded as the cause of the action described by the first clause. In (5.16) and (5.17), *so* is followed by a reference to an action which could be regarded as the effect of the intention described by the first clause. As in the empirical mode, it is the *because* sentence rather than the *so* sentence which conforms to the natural order for an explanation (what is being explained → explanation).

However, in the intentional mode, *so* may be used in the sense of 'in order that' or 'so that' (as in (5.18) and (5.19)) as well as in the sense of 'therefore' (as in (5.16) and (5.17)). I shall refer to the 'in order that' use of *so*, which is specific to the intentional mode, as '$so_{(i)}$'.[2] Either *because* or $so_{(i)}$ may be used to introduce a reason for an action, and the use of either of these connectives will yield a sentence which conforms to the natural order for an explanation. (See examples (5.14) and (5.18), and (5.15) and (5.19).) The difference between *because* and $so_{(i)}$ sentences lies in the way in which the reason is expressed. In a *because* sentence, the reason is expressed by using a phrase which refers to the agent's desire or aim (*wanted to*, *was going to*), whereas in a $so_{(i)}$ sentence, the reason is expressed by using a modal construction (*would...*, *could...*) which refers to the predicted result of the action. Thus, the two types of sentence differ with respect to which of the elements of (5.8) are asserted explicitly and which are presupposed.

There seems to be some relation between the cause/condition distinction, introduced in section 5.1.1, and the linguistic structure of sentences in the intentional mode. For example, constructions involving *because* and *going to* cannot be used when the underlying relation is causal, and constructions involving *so...would* cannot be used when the underlying relation is conditional:

(5.23) *John wound up the toy car because it was going to go.*
(5.24) *Mary took out her crayons so she would do some colouring in.*

5.1.3 *Temporal order in the intentional mode*

In discussing the empirical mode, it is relatively unproblematic to say that causes precede their effects and therefore that *because* is followed by a reference to the event which happened first, whereas *so* is followed by a reference to the event which happened next. On the other hand, in the intentional mode the relationship between causal direction and temporal order is much more complex. In the intentional mode the cause of an action is the agent's intention to achieve a particular result. In one sense, the intention is temporally prior to the action, in that the intention is usually formed before the action is carried out. However, the intention is also 'forward looking' in that it incorporates a prediction about the probable outcome of the action. Therefore, the intention and the action do not form a simple temporal sequence in which the intention comes first. Rather, the intention both precedes the action and 'looks ahead of' the action. Because of this complex relationship between causal direction and temporal order in the intentional mode, it is not helpful to say that *because* is followed by a reference to the event which happened first.

5.1.4 *Exploring children's ability to deal with the intentional mode*

The account presented in the preceding sections suggests that the task of dealing with intentional explanations would be likely to impose a number of demands on the child. First, it is cognitively demanding in that a distinction has to be maintained between the reason–action relation and the action–result relation, and yet these two relations are interdependent. Second, it is linguistically demanding in that the child has to show that he has maintained the distinction between the two types of relation by using a linguistic construction which is appropriate to the intentional mode. If the child confuses the type of construction appropriate to the empirical mode with the type of construction appropriate to the intentional mode, then he will be likely to produce cause–effect inversions, such as:

(5.25) **John wound up the toy car because it went.*

Also, when he is attempting to give intentional explanations, he will tend to produce utterances like:

(5.26) *John wound up the toy car so it went*

which are well-formed but which express an action–result relation rather than an action–reason relation. A further linguistic demand is that the child has to distinguish among *because* constructions, *so* constructions and $so_{(i)}$

constructions, within the intentional mode. Failure to do so would result in the production of inversions, such as:

(5.27) **John wanted the toy car to go because he wound it up.*
(5.28) **John wound up the toy car so he wanted it to go.*
(5.29) **John wound up the toy car because it would go.*

In short, if children are confused either about the distinction between a reason and a result or about the meaning of the causal connectives, then a task involving intentional explanations should give them plenty of opportunities to reveal their confusion by producing cause–effect inversions!

Experiment 5 was designed to investigate 5-year-olds' and 8-year-olds' ability to give intentional explanations. The task used in this experiment involved presenting the child with picture-pairs and telling short stories about them. Each picture-pair depicted an action and a result, and the child's task was to explain the action. Since neither the pictures nor the story made the agent's intention explicit, the child was required to infer the nature of the intention on the basis of the information provided about the result, and on the basis of his knowledge about the action–result relation. Therefore, this particular task demanded a considerable degree of cognitive flexibility on the part of the child. He had to infer the reason for the action on the basis of the result of the action, yet at the same time, he had to maintain a distinction between the reason and the result. The techniques used in eliciting the explanations were to ask the child *Why...?* questions about the actions (e.g. *Why did John wind up the car?*), and (in a later session) to ask the child to complete sentence fragments which referred to the action and which ended in *because* or *so* (e.g. *John wound up the car because...; John wound up the car so...*). Thus, in this particular experiment, the child was required to distinguish between *because* and *so*$_{(i)}$ constructions, but he did not have to deal with *so* in the sense of 'therefore'.

The results of Experiment 5 will be used to address three main issues, which are framed as questions rather than as hypotheses, since we are venturing into an area which is largely unexplored. These issues are:

(1) Is there a developmental progression in the ability to give intentional explanations?
(2) When children express intentional explanations, do they show a preference for a particular linguistic construction, and, if so, is there a developmental change in this preference?
(3) To what extent do children produce cause–effect inversions when attempting to give intentional explanations? Does this vary according to any of the following:
    (a) the age of the children?
    (b) whether the presupposed relation is causal or conditional?

(c) whether the presupposed relation is physical or psychological?

(d) whether the connective is *because* or *so*?

5.2 Method (Experiment 5)

5.2.1 *Subjects*

A total of 48 subjects took part in the experiment. There were 24 subjects in each of two age groups. The mean age for the younger group was 5;10, and the age range was from 5;4 to 6;3. For the older group, the mean age was 8;2 and the ages ranged from 7;9 to 8;6. There were 13 boys and 11 girls in the younger group, and 11 boys and 13 girls in the older group. All the subjects received the questions task, and most of the subjects received the sentence completion task. However, for the younger group the two tasks were separated by the summer vacation, and 4 of the original subjects were not available to take part in the sentence completion task. Therefore, for the sentence completion task, the younger group consisted of 20 subjects with a mean age of 6;1 and an age range from 5;8 to 6;6. In order to equate the two groups for size, 4 of the older subjects were randomly selected to have their data omitted from the analysis of the sentence completion task. The mean age of the older group in the sentence completion task was 8;3, and the age range was from 7;9 to 8;6 (as in the questions task). All the subjects were pupils at a local authority primary school, Musselburgh Burgh.

5.2.2 *Design*

Apart from the exceptions mentioned in the previous section, all the subjects received two tasks: the questions task and the sentence completion task. The questions task was always administered before the sentence completion task. This was done because the questions task was more open-ended than the sentence completion task, and it was important to find out which linguistic construction the children preferred to use before they were influenced by the constraints imposed by the sentence completion task.

For each item in both tasks, the children were presented with two pictures and were told a story. One of the pictures (the top picture) depicted an action and the other picture (the lower picture) depicted a result of the action. The agent's intention was not explicitly mentioned in the story. In the questions task, the subjects were required to answer a *Why?* question about the action depicted in the top picture. In the sentence completion task, the subjects were asked to complete a sentence fragment which described the action depicted in the top picture and which ended in *because* or *so*. This design would probably encourage the production of intentional rather than empirical explanations, since there was no picture depicting a prior causal event. On the other hand, the design would not bias the subjects towards giving non-inverted rather than inverted responses. Both a non-inverted and an inverted response would be likely to be based on the event depicted in the lower picture. However, in order to demonstrate that they intended to express a reason (the inferred intention) rather than a result, the subjects would have to use a linguistic construction appropriate to the intentional mode. In other words, this design means that the children's ability to distinguish between reasons and results is being assessed on the basis of the form rather than the content of their utterances.

The test items were based on twelve stories, each of which was illustrated with two pictures. There were three stories in each of the following categories:

   (i) physical cause
  (ii) psychological cause
 (iii) physical condition
 (iv) psychological condition.

The same stories and pictures were used for both tasks. In the questions task, the subjects were asked twelve *Why?* questions, and in the sentence completion task they were asked to complete six *because* sentences and six *so* sentences. The order of presentation of the stories was constant across subjects and across tasks. The order was random except for the constraint that two consecutive stories could not be from exactly the same category.

The design of the questions task used with the younger age group was slightly different from that used with the older age group. For the younger age group, the questions task was administered over two sessions (on different days). In each session, the subjects received six of the test items involving *Why?* questions and six items involving *Then what...?* questions (e.g. *John wound up the car, didn't he?...Then what happened?*). The stories which were paired with *Why?* questions in one session were paired with *Then what...?* questions in the other session, and the order of presentation was counter-balanced across subjects. Thus, each subject received twelve *Why?* items and twelve *Then what...?* items (relating to the same stories and pictures) over the two sessions. The *Then what...?* questions were included in an attempt to elicit descriptions of the event depicted in the lower picture. By comparing a child's responses to these questions with his responses to the corresponding *Why?* questions, it should be possible to determine whether or not the child is making some distinction between giving a reason and describing a subsequent event, even if he does not employ exactly the same linguistic forms as adults would. However, a preliminary analysis of the results obtained for the younger age group indicated that the children usually did use the same forms as adults. Also, since the children did not always use exactly the same verb in answering the *Why...?* question as in answering the *Then what...?* question, it was difficult to make a systematic comparison between the two sets of responses. For these reasons, the design was modified for the older age group. They received the questions task in a single session. They were asked a *Why?* question about each of the twelve stories which had been used with the younger children. In addition, they were presented with four new stories and were asked a *Then what...?* question about each of these. These four distractor items were interspersed throughout the test items.

In a subsequent session, all the subjects received the sentence completion task. For the younger group, this was the third session and it took place several months after the first two sessions. For the older group, this was the second session and it took place a few days after the first session. For both age groups, the sentence completion task was administered in a single session. It consisted of 16 items: the 12 test items and 4 distractors which involved sentence fragments ending with *and then* (e.g. *Mary turned on the tap and then...*). Two sets of test items were constructed such that each set contained six *because* and six *so* sentence fragments, and such that each story was paired with a *because* fragment in one set and with a *so* fragment in the other set. Half of the subjects in each age group received one set and half received the other set.

5.2.3 *Materials*

The stimulus materials for each item consisted of a story, two pictures and a question or sentence fragment. The general aim in constructing the stories was to make them as natural as possible. Therefore, they included some extra details which were not directly relevant to the task. Each story included a specific reference to the action and the result which were to form the basis of the item, but the agent's intention was not explicitly mentioned. The stories are presented in Appendix 3.

For each story there was a picture depicting the action and a picture depicting the result. The pictures were coloured drawings, and the two pictures for a given story were arranged vertically on a single page. The top picture always depicted the action, and the lower picture always depicted the result. The pages were arranged in a loose-leaf binder.

The questions and sentence fragments are given in Appendix 3. The *Why?* questions were all formed by asking *Why?* about the action depicted in the top picture. Each *Then what..?* question was preceded by a statement describing the action and by a tag question (e.g. *John wound up the car, didn't he?*). For the cause items, the question was: *Then what happened?*, and for the condition items, it was: *Then what did he (she) do?*

5.2.4 *Procedure*

Each child was tested individually in a separate room. The sessions were audio-tape recorded, and were transcribed later. In addition, the experimenter took notes on the child's responses during the testing session.

The picture book was placed in front of the child, and the child was asked to look at the pictures while the experimenter told the story. After each story in the questions task, the experimenter asked the child a *Why?* or *Then what?* question based on the action depicted in the top picture. Before the younger children received their second session, they were told that they would be looking at the same pictures and hearing the same stories again, but that the questions would be 'a little bit different'. Similarly, before the sentence completion task was presented, the older children were told that the pictures and stories would be the same but that 'then we'll do something a little bit different from what we did last time'. All the children received a practice item for the sentence completion task. For this practice item, the subjects were asked to look at a picture while the experimenter told them a story about it. Then, the experimenter read out a sentence fragment (*Tom put his fishing net into the water and he caught . . .*), and said to the subjects, 'Oh, I stopped too soon, didn't I? . . . I want you to help me. When I stop too soon, please will you say the last bit for me? . . . OK. Listen again and then when I stop, you finish it off.' The experimenter repeated the sentence fragment, and, after the subjects had provided a completion, the experimenter asked them to say the complete sentence. ('Now, could you say that all by yourself, please?') If necessary, the experimenter prompted the children with one or more words from the beginning of the sentence. This basic procedure was repeated for each item, except that the subjects usually provided the completion as soon as the experimenter finished the sentence fragment so neither the instructions nor the sentence fragment had to be repeated.

5.2.5 *Questionnaires*

In order to obtain some data on adults' use of intentional explanations, a set of questionnaires was administered to 40 undergraduate students. Each questionnaire contained twelve items which corresponded to the test items presented to the children, and the stories on which the items were based. There were three types of questionnaire, and each student completed only one of these. In Questionnaire I, the twelve items were the *Why?* questions which had been presented to the children. Twenty students completed this questionnaire. Questionnaire IIa consisted of one of the sets of sentence completion items, and Questionnaire IIb consisted of the other set. Each of these questionnaires was completed by ten students.

5.3 Analysis of results

The data for each child consisted of three types of response: responses to *Why?* questions, sentence completions, and attempts to produce the whole sentence. These responses were coded using seven categories:

A. No response

B. Temporal expressions: The responses in this category referred to events or states which were subsequent to the actions, but they did not involve the use of causal connectives. Examples of such responses are:

(5.30) *Mary put on a silly nose and showed John it.*
(5.31) *John washed his hands and then went down to his tea.*
(5.32) *Mary took out her crayons then she went and coloured in.*

C. Rule-based explanations: The responses in this category explained the action by referring to a rule, regularity or convention. They usually involved the use of *if* or *when* and present tense verb forms, as in the following example:

(5.33) E: *Why did John wash his hands?*
        S: *'Cos when you eat, it you don't wash your hands you get germs in your food.*

D. Non-intentional explanations: The responses in this category were appropriate as explanations but they were not in the intentional mode. This category included appropriate empirical explanations and responses which consisted of *for* followed by a noun-phrase. The following are examples of responses in the non-intentional category:

(5.34) E: *Mary put on a pretty dress because...*
        S: *'Cos it was someone's birthday.*
(5.35) E: *Mary put on a silly nose so...*
        S: *She scared Tom.*
(5.36) E: *Why did John buy a bunch of flowers?*
        S: *For his Gran.*

E. Inversions: A response was assigned to this category if there was a clash between the direction of the causal relation specified by the connective and the direction of the causal relation indicated by the content of the clauses. If *because* was followed by a reference to an effect or result which was not appropriately marked as being in the intentional mode, then the response was

93

classed as an inversion. Similarly, if *so* was followed by a reference to a cause or reason which was not marked as being an aim or intention, then the response was classed as an inversion. Responses in which the type of linguistic construction appropriate to a *because* sentence in the intentional mode was confused with the type of linguistic construction appropriate to a *so*$_{(i)}$ sentence in the intentional mode were also included in the inversions category. Here are some examples of responses which were classed as inversions:

(5.37) E: *Why did John wind up the car?*
　　　　S: *'Cos it went away.*
(5.38) E: *Mary put some money into the machine so…*
　　　　S: *She wanted a bar of chocolate.*
(5.39) E: *Mary took out her crayons because…*
　　　　S: *She could draw a picture.*
(5.40) E: *Mary put on a pretty dress so…*
　　　　S: *She was going to go to a party after lunch.*

F. *Possible inversions/tense errors:* The status of the responses in this category is ambiguous. These are responses in which *so* was used along with a present tense modal, *will* or *can*, as in:

(5.41) E: *Why did John water the bulbs?*
　　　　S: *So they'll grow.*

Such responses could be interpreted either as evidence that the child could not distinguish appropriately between reasons and results, or as evidence that he had not mastered the tense rules but was attempting to give an intentional explanation (*so they would grow*).

G. *Intentional explanations:* In order to be included in this category, a response had to constitute an explanation of the action in terms of the agent's intention to achieve a particular effect. In addition, the response had to employ a linguistic construction which was appropriate to the intentional mode. The responses in this category were sub-categorised according to the type of linguistic construction which they employed. There were five such categories:

(1) Infinitive: e.g. *John wound up the toy car to make it go.*
(2) *Because…wanted to…:* e.g. *John wound up the toy car because he wanted it to go.*
(3) *Because…was going to…:* e.g. *Mary took out her crayons because she was going to do some colouring in.*
(4) *So…would…:* e.g. *John wound up the toy car so (that) it would go.*
(5) *So…could…:* e.g. *Mary took out her crayons so (that) she could colour in.*

5.4 Results

5.4.1 *The ability to give intentional explanations*

Table 21 shows the frequency and percentage of responses assigned to each of the main categories. The results indicate that the children showed a strong tendency to produce intentional explanations. For both age groups and for all the tasks, most of the responses were in the intentional category. It is important to note that the intentional category includes only non-inverted intentional responses. Therefore, the children were not only attempting to produce intentional explanations. They were also succeeding in producing a large percentage of well-formed intentional explanations.

The percentages of intentional responses for the adult group were 97% for the questions task (Questionnaire 1) and 95% for the sentence completion task (Questionnaires 11a and 11b). Thus, the adults' tendency to produce intentional explanations was slightly stronger than the children's.

The fact that the 5-year-olds produced fewer intentional responses than the 8-year-olds in the sentence completion and whole sentence tasks may indicate that the younger children are less able to produce intentional explanations without the support of *Why?* questions than the older children are. On the other hand, since the time interval between the questions task and the sentence completion task was much shorter for the older group than for the younger group, it is possible that, in the sentence completion task, the older children were simply being influenced by the way they had responded in the questions task. In any case, the results for the questions task indicate that, under favourable conditions, even 5-year-olds can demonstrate a considerable ability to give intentional explanations.

5.4.2 *Preferred linguistic constructions*

As the results presented in Table 22 show, the linguistic construction which was used most frequently in the questions task was the infinitive construction. For the sentence completion task, the responses were distributed much more evenly among the various linguistic constructions. This indicates that the children were taking account of the constraints of the task. Although they preferred using the infinitive, they could be encouraged to use the other constructions. The whole sentence task imposes fewer constraints than the sentence completion task but more constraints than the questions task. It is interesting that the percentage of infinitive construction responses for the whole sentence task is greater than for the sentence completion task but less than for the questions task. When the constraints of the task were relaxed, the children tended to return to using their preferred construction.

Table 21. *Frequency and percentage of responses assigned to each category*

	No response		Temporal		Rule-based		Non-intentional		Inversions		Inversion/tense error		Intentional	
	f	%	f	%	f	%	f	%	f	%	f	%	f	%
5-year-olds														
Questions (N = 24)	1	0.35	0	0	2	0.69	34	11.80	15	5.21	3	1.04	233	80.90
Sentence completion (N = 20)	0	0	0	0	0	0	55	22.92	24	10	4	1.67	157	65.42
Whole sentence (N = 20)	0	0	57	23.75	0	0	22	9.17	7	2.92	1	0.42	153	63.75
8-year-olds														
Questions (N = 24)	0	0	0	0	10	3.47	37	12.85	5	1.74	0	0	236	81.94
Sentence completion (N = 20)	0	0	0	0	3	1.25	25	10.41	12	5	1	0.42	199	82.92
Whole sentence (N = 20)	1	0.42	16	6.67	3	1.25	19	7.92	3	1.25	1	0.42	197	82.08

Percentages calculated on the basis of the total number of responses per age group per task.

Table 22. Linguistic constructions used in giving intentional responses: frequencies and percentages (of total number of intentional responses per age group per task)

	Because + going to		Because + want to		so (as) (that) + could		so (as) (that) + would		INFINITIVE		OTHER	
	f	%	f	%	f	%	f	%	f	%	f	%
5-year-olds												
Questions	9	3.86	19	8.15	31	13.30	22	9.44	147	63.09	5	2.14
Sentence completion	19	12.10	42	26.75	43	27.39	32	20.38	21	13.38	0	0
Whole sentence	7	4.58	23	15.03	50	32.68	26	16.99	47	30.72	0	0
8-year-olds												
Questions	19	8.05	23	9.74	36	15.25	37	15.68	115	48.73	6	2.54
Sentence completion	17	8.54	49	24.62	52	26.13	44	22.11	36	18.09	1	0.5
Whole sentence	15	7.61	41	20.81	46	23.35	40	20.30	54	27.41	1	0.51

Table 23. *Linguistic constructions used by adults in giving intentional responses: frequencies and percentages (of total number of intentional responses per task)*

	Because + going to		Because + want to		so (as) (that) + could		so (as) (that) + would		INFINITIVE		OTHER	
	f	%	f	%	f	%	f	%	f	%	f	%
Questions	21	9.01	16	6.87	12	5.15	16	6.87	160	68.67	8	3.43
Sentence completion	25	10.96	81	35.53	69	30.26	40	17.54	0	0	13	5.70

Table 24. *Comparison between number of subjects preferring 'because' and number preferring 'so' in giving intentional explanations in questions task (sign test)*

	Prefer *because*	Prefer *so*	No preference	
5 years	5	12	7	NS
8 years	8	11	5	NS
Adults	10	5	5	NS

A similar pattern emerges from the adult data, as Table 23 indicates. The infinitive construction was preferred in the questions task, but not in the sentence completion task. The fact that none of the adults' responses to the sentence completion task used the infinitive construction, whereas some of the children's responses did, is probably due to an increase with age in the ability to take account of the constraints of the task. However, some caution is required in drawing such a conclusion. The adult subjects came from a more highly selected sample than the children did, in that the adults were all university undergraduates. Also, the fact that the adults received a written version of the task may have helped them to attend to the particular connective which was used in each sentence fragment.

In view of the finding that performance was better for *because* than for *so* sentences in the causal task based on the empirical mode, it is important to compare *because* and *so* sentences in the intentional mode. In the questions task, when the subjects had a free choice as to the linguistic construction they used, did they show a preference for either *because* or *so?* As the results presented in Table 24 indicate, there were no significant differences between the number of subjects preferring *because* and the number preferring *so.*

5.4.3 *Occurrence of inversions*

The results which were presented in Table 21 indicate that inversions account for only a very small percentage of the children's responses, whereas non-inverted intentional responses account for the majority of the children's responses. However, the results in Table 22 show that many of these intentional responses involve the use of the infinitive construction. It is difficult to see how the children could produce cause–effect inversions while using an infinitive construction. Therefore, it is only when the children are using *because* or *so* constructions that their ability to avoid inversions is really put to the test. Table 25 presents the results of a comparison between the mean number of inversions and the mean number of intentional responses using *because* or *so* constructions. For both age groups and for all the tasks,

Table 25. *Comparison between mean number of inversions and mean number of intentional responses using 'because' or 'so'*

	Inverted	Intentional (because/so)
Questions		
5 years	0.75	3.42
8 years	0.21	4.79
Sentence completion		
5 years	1.40	6.80
8 years	0.65	8.10
Whole sentence		
5 years	0.40	5.30
8 years	0.20	7.10

Maximum possible per cell = 12.

Table 26. *Frequency of inversions (and possible inversions) for each category of item*

	Physical cause	Psychological cause	Physical condition	Psychological condition
Questions				
5-year-olds	11	3	0	4
8-year-olds	1	1	0	3
Sentence completion				
5-year-olds	7	11	6	4
8-year-olds	3	4	2	4
Whole sentence				
5-year-olds	3	4	0	1
8-year-olds	1	1	0	2
Totals	26	24	8	18
	50		26	

there were more intentional responses using *because* or *so* than there were inversions. This result was obtained despite the fact that the inverted category includes the possible inversions/tense errors, and despite the fact that some of the inversions may have resulted from attempts to produce non-intentional rather than intentional explanations whereas the non-inverted responses all come from the intentional category.[3]

Although the inversion rate is low for both age groups, the results in Table 25 suggest that it is even lower for the 8-year-olds than for the 5-year-olds.

Table 27. *Comparison between 'because' and 'so' items (in sentence completion and whole sentence tasks) with respect to mean number of inversions*

	Because	So	
Sentence completion			
5 years	0.85	0.55	NS
8 years	0.30	0.35	NS
Whole sentence			
5 years	0.25	0.15	NS
8 years	0.15	0.005	NS

Wilcoxon matched-pairs signed-ranks tests, 2-tailed. Maximum possible per cell = 6.

A Mann-Whitney U test indicated that the age effect was statistically significant for the questions task ($p < 0.05$) and the sentence completion task ($p < 0.02$), but not for the whole sentence task. The lack of a significant age effect for the whole sentence task may be partly attributable to the fact that many of the 5-year-olds' responses to this task were in the temporal category. (See Table 21.)

Table 26 shows how the inversions and possible inversions were distributed among the four categories of item. There is a slight trend towards the frequency of inversions being greater for cause items than for condition items. However, this can only be suggestive since the total number of inversions is so small.

In Table 27, *because* and *so* items (in the sentence completion and whole sentence tasks) are compared with respect to the mean number of inversions. Wilcoxon matched-pairs signed-ranks tests indicated that none of the differences was significant. A similar result was obtained for the questions task (on the basis of a sign test).

5.5 Discussion

In their explanations of actions in terms of intentions, the subjects in this experiment demonstrated considerable linguistic and cognitive abilities. Both the 5-year-olds and the 8-year-olds were able to infer the agent's intention on the basis of knowledge about the action and the result. This finding is congruent with Stein and Trabasso's finding (1982) that children of these ages can make inferences about motives on the basis of various types of information contained in stories. The children in the present study also showed an ability to distinguish between the reason for an action and the result of an action, despite the fact that they had to infer the reason on the basis of their knowledge of the result. This is strong evidence that the children are capable of a considerable degree of cognitive flexibility. It is also evidence that the children's understanding of psychological causality has a systematic basis. They are not confused about what is a reason and what is a result. Thus, their reasoning about psychological causality is not as immature as Piaget implies it is.

The children were also able to mark the distinction between a reason and a result linguistically. Although the children (like the adults) preferred to use the infinitive construction to mark their explanations as being in the intentional mode, they also demonstrated an ability to use *because* and *so* constructions appropriately, in that they produced significantly more non-inverted intentional responses than inverted responses when they were using *because* and *so* constructions. This finding lends further support to the argument that the child's use and understanding of the causal connectives are guided by knowledge other than the knowledge that *because* is followed by a reference to the first event whereas *so* is followed by a reference to the second event. This knowledge about temporal order would not be particularly useful for dealing with sentences in the intentional mode, since there is a complex relationship between causal direction and temporal order in the intentional mode. The child's knowledge can be more appropriately characterised in terms of causal direction.

In Chapter 4, it was argued that children know that *because* is followed by a cause, and that they have a notion of 'plausible cause'. The present findings suggest that children know that an agent's desire or aim to achieve a particular result constitutes a plausible cause for an action. Shultz (1980) argues that young children view intentions as important causes of human behaviour, and to support his argument he presents evidence that by the age of 5 years children have a very good grasp of the concept of intention. For example, his research has demonstrated that young children can distinguish intended actions from non-intended behaviours. As Shultz admits, his research programme constitutes a rather indirect approach to the issue of whether children view intentions as causes. Having an adequate concept of intention is a necessary but not a sufficient condition for explaining behaviour in terms of intentions. The present experiment adopted a more direct approach by actually asking children to explain actions, and the results lend further support to Shultz's argument.

In addition, the results of this experiment indicate that children know that in the intentional mode either *because* or $so_{(i)}$ can be used to introduce the reason for an action, but that if *because* is used, the explanation has to focus on the agent's aim or desire, whereas if $so_{(i)}$ is used, the explanation has to focus on the predicted result of the action. This distinction is illustrated by the following pair of sentences:

(5.42) *John wound up the car because he wanted it to go.*

(5.43) *John wound up the car so it would go.*

(See section 5.1.2.)

The results of Experiment 4 suggested that children know that *because* introduces a cause before they know that *so* introduces an effect. However, the results of Experiment 5 provide no evidence of a similar asymmetry between *because* and $so_{(i)}$. The children did not show a preference for using *because* constructions rather than $so_{(i)}$ constructions. (In fact, they tended to use $so_{(i)}$ slightly more than *because*, but the effect was not significant). Nor did they produce more inversions for $so_{(i)}$ sentences than for *because* sentences. The distinction between *because* and $so_{(i)}$ in the intentional mode seems rather more subtle than the distinction between *because* and *so* in the empirical mode. Therefore, the finding that children can deal with $so_{(i)}$ in the intentional mode at an earlier age than they can deal with *so* in the empirical mode may seem rather surprising. However, the finding may be attributable to the fact that $so_{(i)}$ sentences, like *because* sentences, conform to the natural order for an explanation. (See section 4.1.2.) In contrast, when *so* is used in the sense of 'therefore', the natural order for an explanation is violated. It may be that children begin by learning the 'more natural' uses of the causal connectives.

In this chapter, we have seen how our picture of the child's knowledge of the causal connectives' meaning can be enriched when we consider intentional explanations as well as empirical explanations. In the next chapter, I shall elaborate further on this picture by investigating explanations in the deductive mode.

6   The deductive mode

6.1 Introduction

6.1.1 *Explanations in the deductive mode*

In the deductive mode, a judgement or conclusion is explained or justified in terms of some form of evidence.[1] The evidence may be observable, or it may take the form of a rule or of a 'given' fact. The role of the causal connectives in deductive sentences is to make explicit the links in the deductive process, rather than the causal relations between events. However, a deductive explanation may draw on the speaker's knowledge of the types of causal relations between events which are made explicit in empirical explanations. For example, the deductive explanation expressed by the sentence:

(6.1) *We can tell that John has a broken leg because it is in plaster*

presupposes the physical relation which is made explicit in the sentence:

(6.2) *John's leg is in plaster because it is broken.*

Similarly, the deductive sentence:

(6.3) *We can tell that Mary is sad because she is crying*

presupposes the psychological relation expressed by:

(6.4) *Mary is crying because she is sad.*

Thus, deductive explanations may have physical content (as in (6.1)) or psychological content (as in (6.3)). Alternatively, they may have logical content, as in:

(6.5) *We can tell that half nine is not four because four and four make eight.*

Most of the previous research on children's understanding of the causal connectives has either been based solely on the empirical mode or has compared empirical sentences to deductive sentences with logical content. This has resulted in our picture of the child's knowledge of the connectives' meaning being not simply incomplete but distorted, since there is a complex relationship between the linguistic structure of deductive sentences and that of empirical sentences.

6.1.2 *Linguistic analysis of sentences in the deductive mode*

As the following sentences illustrate, in the deductive mode *because* is used to introduce the evidence on which a conclusion is based, whereas *so* is used to introduce the conclusion:

(6.6) *We can tell that John has a broken leg because it is in plaster.*
(6.7) *John's leg is in plaster so we can tell that he has a broken leg.*

If the evidence is regarded as the 'cause' of the conclusion, then the deductive and empirical uses of the connectives appear to be rather similar. In both cases, *because* introduces a cause, whereas *so* introduces an effect. However, the situation is complicated by the fact that the clause which is used to refer to the cause of a conclusion in a deductive sentence may be used to refer to an effect in an empirical sentence, such as:

(6.8) *John's leg is in plaster because it is broken.*

Thus, the fact that John's leg is in plaster may be regarded either as the effect of John's leg being broken or as evidence for the conclusion that John's leg is broken. However, these alternatives are not really mutually exclusive, since a deductive sentence (such as (6.6)) presupposes the relation which would be expressed by the corresponding empirical sentence ((6.8)). When the deductive sentence has logical content, there is no need to draw a distinction between the relation which is expressed and the relation which is presupposed. The only relation involved is the logical or deductive relation.

When the content of a *because* or *so* sentence is non-logical, it is not possible to determine the truth-value of the sentence unless one knows whether the sentence is to be interpreted in terms of the empirical or the deductive mode. For example, while it is true that 'John's leg being in plaster' could be the cause of the conclusion that 'John's leg is broken,' it would probably be false to say that 'John's leg being in plaster is the cause of John's leg being broken.'

The examples which we have considered so far suggest that empirical sentences can be distinguished from deductive sentences on the basis of their linguistic form. The deductive sentences contain the phrase *we can tell that*, whereas the empirical sentences do not. However, the following sentences could also be used to give deductive explanations:

(6.9) *John has a broken leg because it is in plaster.*
(6.10) *John's leg is in plaster so he has a broken leg.*

These sentences can be regarded as elliptical versions of sentences (6.6) and

(6.7). Sentences like (6.6) and (6.7) are explicitly deductive in that they contain a phrase (*we can tell that*) which indicates that a conclusion is being expressed. There are a number of ways of making a sentence explicitly deductive, and some of these are illustrated by the following sentences:

(6.11) *We know that John has a broken leg because it is in plaster.*
(6.12) *I think John has a broken leg because it is in plaster.*
(6.13) *John must have a broken leg because it is in plaster.*
(6.14) *John's leg is in plaster so it might be broken.*
(6.15) *John's leg is in plaster so perhaps it's broken.*

Each of these sentences contains a phrase which refers to the speaker's propositional attitude towards the conclusion: a phrase which expresses the speaker's degree of commitment to the truth of the conclusion. Such phrases (*know that, think, must, might, perhaps,* etc.) will be termed 'deductive markers'. When a deductive marker is not present, as in sentences (6.9) and (6.10), the form of the sentence does not enable us to decide whether the sentence should be interpreted in terms of the empirical mode or in terms of the deductive mode. In other words, such sentences are potentially ambiguous.

Furthermore, even a sentence (such as (6.6)) which contains a deductive marker is potentially ambiguous. The two alternative readings of sentence (6.6) can be informally represented as:

(6.16) [*We can tell that* [*John has a broken leg*]] – because – [*it is in plaster*].
(6.17) *We can tell that* [[*John has a broken leg*] – because – [*it is in plaster*]].

The reading in (6.16) corresponds to the deductive use of *because*, whereas the reading in (6.17) corresponds to the empirical use of *because*. With this particular content, only the deductive reading yields an acceptable sentence. However, the plausibility of the empirical reading becomes apparent when the content of the final clause is altered to give:

(6.18) *We can tell that* [[*John has a broken leg*] – because – [*he fell off his bike*]].

On the other hand, sentences (such as (6.7)) which contain *so* and a deductive marker (rather than *because* and a deductive marker) seem to be unambiguously in the deductive mode.

Sentences (6.6), (6.9) and (6.10) have been described as '*potentially ambiguous*' in order to leave open the question of whether or not speakers and hearers are actually aware of the ambiguities. There are a number of 'disambiguating factors' which might serve to reduce awareness of the ambiguities, or which might help hearers to decide which of the alternative readings is more plausible if they are aware of an ambiguity.

Introduction

One type of disambiguating factor consists of the information which the linguistic and non-linguistic context provides about the speaker's probable aims. For example, in the context of a discussion about what the present state of the weather is, a deductive reading of the following sentence would seem more plausible than an empirical reading:

(6.19) *It is windy because the branches are moving.*

On the other hand, if the same sentence was produced in the context of a discussion about the physical laws underlying meteorological phenomena, then the hearer might be more likely to adopt the empirical reading (and to conclude that the speaker did not understand the phenomenon she was trying to explain). A second possible type of disambiguating factor is the form of the causal sentence such as whether or not it contains a deductive marker. A third type of disambiguating factor is related to the content of the causal sentence. For example, a hearer may be more likely to interpret sentence (6.20) in terms of the deductive mode than in terms of the empirical mode:

(6.20) *John has a broken leg because it is in plaster.*

On the other hand, she may prefer an interpretation based on the empirical mode for the sentence:

(6.21) *John has a broken leg because he fell off his bike.*

This would suggest that the hearer is working on the assumption that the speaker will usually produce sentences which are true and well-formed. On the basis of this assumption, the hearer would then use her world knowledge to select an interpretation which yields an acceptable rather than an unacceptable sentence.

It seems likely that these three types of disambiguating factor will interact with one another in a complex way. Sometimes they may reinforce one another, and sometimes they may be in competition with one another. However, for present purposes, the most important point is that some type of disambiguation is frequently required. Causal sentences have to be interpreted in terms of a particular explanatory mode, yet the distinction between the deductive mode and the empirical mode is not always clear-cut.

6.1.3 *Inversions and the empirical/deductive distinction*

The potential ambiguity of *because* and *so* sentences presents a problem for the type of linguistic analysis which has guided most of the previous experimental work on children's understanding of the causal connectives. The assumption has been that inversions can be defined (and detected) on the basis of the superficial form and content of the sentences. An inversion is said to have occurred if *because* is followed by a reference to an effect, or if *so* is followed by a reference to a cause (where 'cause' and 'effect' are interpreted in terms of the empirical mode). Therefore, sentences such as the following would be classed as inversions:

(6.22) *John has a broken leg because it is in plaster.*
(6.23) *John's leg is in plaster so he has broken leg.*

However, if these sentences were interpreted in terms of the deductive mode (as the linguistic analysis outlined in section 6.1.2 suggests they could be), then they would be regarded as elliptical versions of (6.24) and (6.25), and therefore as acceptable:

(6.24) *We can tell that John has a broken leg because it is in plaster.*
(6.25) *John's leg is in plaster so we can tell that he has a broken leg.*

Piaget (1926, 1928) does show some appreciation of this problem, when he notes that children's inversions sometimes give the appearance that they are producing justifications rather than explanations.[2] However, Piaget immediately dismisses the problem by saying that the children are not actually trying to give justifications, but are simply expressing the first relation which occurs to them irrespective of its nature. Piaget gives four main reasons for this claim, and they are all related to his more general claim that the young child's thinking is egocentric. First, he argues that young children, because of their egocentrism, simply do not see any need to justify their judgements. If something is obvious to them, then they assume that it will be obvious to everyone else. Second, he claims that, before the age of about 7 or 8, children's tendency to psychologise leads them to confuse relations of physical causality with logical relations, and to view them both as psychological relations. Third, he claims that young children's thinking lacks direction, and therefore that young children are incapable of distinguishing between causes and consequences. Piaget argues that justification cannot have an 'autonomous existence' until children are able to distinguish between causes and consequences, and among physical, psychological and logical relations. Fourth, Piaget found, in his sentence completion experiments, that children were less good at completing the sentences which required a justification (e.g. *Half nine is not four because...*) than they were at completing the sentences which required an empirical explanation (e.g. *I shan't go to school tomorrow because...*).

Piaget's position can be challenged on a number of grounds. In the first place, there is an element of circularity in his argument. He argues that the child's tendency to produce inversions is evidence that the child cannot differentiate between causes and consequences and therefore that justification cannot have an autonomous existence. This, in turn, means that the child's inversions cannot be accounted for by saying that the child was aiming to give a justification when the experimenter was expecting an explanation. A second reason for challenging Piaget's position is that the evidence reported in this book argues against the claim that young children tend to psychologise and to confuse causes with effects. Finally, Piaget's finding that performance was poor on sentence completion items requiring justifications should be interpreted with caution. The sentences which required a justification were also the sentences which had logical content, so it is possible that the children's poor performance was due to an inability to deal with logical content rather than to an inability (or reluctance) to give justifications.

For these reasons, it is important to give further consideration to children's ability to deal with deductive explanations and also to the question of the interpretation of inversions. The fact that the truth-value of *because* and *so* sentences is dependent on the mode of explanation and that the empirical/ deductive distinction is not always clear-cut may pose problems for children who are trying to grasp the meaning of the causal connectives. They may find it difficult to draw a distinction between the two modes, or they may not realise that *because* and *so* are used in different ways in the different modes. Those of us who are trying to understand the child's knowledge of the connectives' meaning will also encounter problems if we do not consider the relationship between the explanatory mode and the way the connectives are used and understood, for we will be in danger of misrepresenting the nature of the child's task. Therefore, it is important to investigate the way children and adults deal with causal sentences in the deductive mode, both in order to obtain a better picture of the nature of the child's task and in order to assess the child's success in coping with that task.

6.1.4 *Temporal order in the deductive mode*

In Chapter 5, it was argued that intentional sentences would pose problems for a linguistic analysis which emphasises the causal connectives' role as indicators of temporal order. A similar argument can be advanced regarding deductive sentences. For a deductive sentence, 'temporal order' could be taken as referring either to the order of the stages in the deductive process or to the order of the events/states which provide the subject-matter for the deduction. If we assume that the order of the stages in the deductive process is 'evidence → conclusion', then we could say that *because* is followed by a reference to the first stage whereas *so* is followed by a reference to the second stage. However, the assumption that the deductive process operates from evidence to conclusion can be challenged on the grounds that a person may sometimes start with the conclusion and then look around for some supporting evidence. Evans, Barston and Pollard (1983) found that when adults were asked to think aloud while carrying out reasoning tasks, they were as likely to mention the conclusion before the premises as to mention the premises before the conclusion. It therefore seems more appropriate to say that *because* introduces the evidence whereas *so* introduces the conclusion, than to attempt to define *because* and *so* in terms of the temporal order of the stages in the deductive process.

Further complexities arise when we consider the temporal order of the events/states which provide the subject-matter for the deduction. The evidence can be used to make an inference about a prior, a future, or a simultaneous event/state. Here are some examples of sentences which fall into each of these categories:

Prior:

(6.26) *There's a puddle on the floor so we can tell that Mary spilt the milk.*
(6.27) *We can tell that Mary spilt the milk because there's a puddle on the floor.*

Future:

(6.28) *The bridge is collapsing so the car will fall into the river.*
(6.29) *The car will fall into the river because the bridge is collapsing.*

Simultaneous:

(6.30) *John's leg is in plaster so we can tell that he has a broken leg.*
(6.31) *We can tell that John has a broken leg because it is in plaster.*

As these examples show, the rule that *because* is followed by a reference to the first event/state and *so* is followed by a reference to the second event/state holds only for the 'future' category. This rule is irrelevant to the 'simultaneous' category, and is in conflict with the way in which the connectives are used in the 'prior' category.[3]

While it is evident that the temporal order of the underlying events/states cannot be used to give an adequate account of the semantics of deductive sentences, it would be interesting nevertheless to investigate whether the underlying temporal order has any effect on performance. In the present experiments, investigation of this issue will be restricted to a comparison between deductions about prior events/states and deductions about simultaneous events/states. If the children are relying on an order-of-mention strategy, then they should exhibit a random pattern of responding to the simultaneous items. In contrast, for prior items, they should show a systematic response pattern consisting of correct responses to deductive *because* items and empirical *so* items and incorrect responses to deductive *so* items and empirical *because* items. (The order-of-mention coincides with the temporal order of the events/states for deductive *because* and empirical *so* sentences, but not for deductive *so* and empirical *because* sentences.)

6.1.5 *Assessing knowledge of the deductive mode*

The main aims of the two experiments reported in this chapter were to assess the extent to which children can distinguish between the empirical and deductive modes, and to investigate children's ability to use the causal connectives in a way appropriate to the deductive mode. Adult control groups were included in both experiments since the linguistic analysis outlined in section 6.1.2 suggests that the distinction between the modes may not be clear-cut even for adults.

Experiment 6, the Deductive/Empirical experiment, assessed the subjects' ability to distinguish between the modes on the basis of linguistic cues provided by the experimenter. The subjects in one condition (the questions condition) were asked to answer *Why...?* and *How do you know...?* questions, and the subjects in a second condition (the sentence completion condition) were asked to complete sentence fragments of the form *B because...* and of the form *We can tell that B because...* If the subjects consistently responded to the *Why...?/B because...* items by referring to the cause of the event/state mentioned in the item, and to the *How do you know...?/We can tell that B because...* items by referring to the evidence for the conclusion mentioned in the item, then this would indicate that they were able to distinguish between the empirical and deductive modes.

In Experiment 7, the Deductive Marking experiment, a context was set up which would be likely to encourage the subjects to produce deductive explanations so that their use of deductive markers and of the causal connectives could be investigated. If the subjects used deductive markers to show that they were talking about conclusions rather than events, then this would indicate that they were able to distinguish between the empirical and deductive modes. If the subjects consistently used *so* to introduce a conclusion and *because* to introduce the evidence for a conclusion, then this would indicate that they knew how to use the causal connectives in the deductive mode. Such a finding, when combined with the findings of Experiment 4, would also suggest that the subjects were able to distinguish between the empirical and deductive modes, since the connectives are used differently in the two modes. Thus, Experiment 7 investigated the extent to which the subjects would show an understanding of the deductive/empirical distinction through their *use* of language when they were cued into the deductive mode by the context.

6.2 Experiment 6: The Deductive/Empirical experiment – hypotheses

The linguistic analysis presented in section 6.1.2 implies that the task of distinguishing between the deductive and empirical modes on the basis of the deductive markers is likely to be a difficult one for the young child. There are three main reasons for this potential difficulty. First, deductive markers seem to be optional rather than obligatory in deductive mode sentences. Second, even when deductive markers occur, they seem to interact with contextual cues to determine the truth-value of the sentences. Third, the deductive mode is parasitic on the empirical mode: this is likely to contribute to the difficulty of distinguishing the two modes and also to make mastery of the deductive mode lag behind mastery of the empirical mode. Hence, the main hypotheses for Experiment 6 were that the ability to distinguish between the deductive and empirical modes on the basis of linguistic cues would increase with age, and that children's performance would be better for empirical items than for deductive items. However, it was also predicted that, even for adults, the deductive/empirical distinction would not be totally clear-cut.

The effect of temporal order was investigated by comparing 'simultaneous' items with 'prior' items. If the subjects were following an order-of-mention strategy, it would be expected that they would respond randomly to the simultaneous items, while for the prior items they would give correct responses to the deductive items and incorrect responses to the empirical items. On the other hand, the findings and arguments which have been presented in this book so far would lead one to expect that the temporal order factor would not affect performance.

To investigate the effect of content, sentences with physical content were compared with sentences with psychological content. (There were no items with logical content in this experiment since it is not possible to have empirical sentences with logical content.) Previous research would lead one to expect that performance might be better on psychological items than on physical items. On the other hand, the findings reported in this book would lead one to expect that performance would not vary according to the type of content.

Since the sentence fragments used in the sentence completion task are potentially ambiguous, whereas the questions used in the questions task are not, it was predicted that the subjects would be better at distinguishing between the deductive and empirical modes in the questions task than in the sentence completion task.

6.3 Method

6.3.1 *Subjects*

There were 32 children in each of three age groups: 5-year-olds, 8-year-olds and 10-year-olds. The mean ages and age ranges for each of these groups were as follows: 5;6 (5;0 to 6;0), 8;3 (7;9 to 8;8) and 10;5 (10;0 to 10;11). The 5-year-old group consisted of 17 boys and 15 girls, the 8-year-old group consisted of 20 boys and 12 girls, and the 10-year-old group consisted of 16 boys and 16 girls. All the children were pupils at the same local authority primary school (Trinity Primary, Edinburgh).

There were 56 adult subjects who were all undergraduates. Sixteen of these subjects completed a questionnaire which asked them to judge the acceptability of sentences. The remainder of the adult subjects received written versions of the tasks presented to the children.

6.3.2 *Design*

Half of the subjects in each age group received the questions task and half received the sentence completion task. The items for both tasks were based on the same set of 16 sequences. Each sequence consists of three elements; $A \to B \to C$, where A is the cause of B and C corresponds to the evidence for the occurrence of B. One deductive item and one empirical item were derived from each sequence. In the questions task the deductive items were of the form *How do you know B?*, and the empirical items were of the form *Why B?* In the sentence completion task the deductive items were of the form *We can tell that B because...*, and the empirical items were of the form *B because...* For both tasks, the predicted response was (*because*) C for the deductive items and (*because*) A for the empirical items. The deductive/empirical variable was a within-subjects variable. Each child received 32 items, of which 16 were deductive and 16 were empirical.

The temporal order and content variables were also within-subjects. For half of the items which each subject received, the relation between B and C was simultaneous, and for the other half it was sequential (and inferences about prior events/states were required). Within each of these categories, half of the items involved physical relations between A and B and between B and C, and half involved psychological relations between A and B and between B and C.

The total set of 32 items was divided into two parallel subsets. Each subset contained one item based on each of the 16 sequences. If the deductive item based on a given sequence was assigned to subset A, then the empirical item based on that sequence would be assigned to subset B and vice versa. Within each subset, half of the items in each of the temporal order and content categories were deductive and half were empirical. (See Appendix 4.) The children received two sessions, with one subset being presented in the first session and the other in the second session. The order of presentation of the subsets was counter-balanced within each age group and within each type of task. The adult subjects received only one subset of items. Half of the adults in each task condition received subset A and the other half received subset B. All the children and adults received the items within each subset in the same random order. This order was also the same for both subsets, apart from the fact that the items which were deductive in one subset were empirical in the other subset.

The acceptability judgement questionnaire consisted of 16 items. (See Appendix 5.) For each item, there were four sentences with the following forms:

> *B because A.*
> *B because C.*
> *We can tell that B because C.*
> *We can tell that B because A.*

The content of the items was the same as the content of the items presented to the children. The subject's task was to rank the four sentences according to their acceptability. The order of presentation of the four types of sentence was varied randomly across items, but was the same for all the subjects.

6.3.3 *Procedure*

For each item (in both tasks) the child was presented with two coloured pictures corresponding to elements A and C of the sequence. The pictures were placed side by side on the table in front of the child. The picture corresponding to A was always on the left of the picture corresponding to C. The experimenter gave a brief description of each picture, and pointed to each picture as she described it. Picture A was always described before Picture C. (The descriptions of the pictures are presented in Appendix 4.)

In the questions task, the experimenter asked a tag question about B, and then asked the critical question which was of the form *Why B?* for empirical items and *How do you know B?* for deductive items. For example, in one item the child was shown a picture of John falling off his bike (A) and a picture of John with his leg in plaster (C). The tag question about B was:

(6.32) *John has a broken leg, hasn't he?*

and this was followed by either:

(6.33) *Why does John have a broken leg?*

or:

(6.34) *How do you know John has a broken leg?*

Thus, the pictures and descriptions provided information only about elements A and C. This procedure was adopted in order to create a context in which B would have to be inferred, and therefore in which deductive questions would seem reasonably natural. However, it seems odd to ask a *Why?* question about a particular event/state when the occurrence of that event/state is not 'given'.

Therefore, the tag question was included in case the child had not actually made the expected inference.

At the beginning of the first session for the sentence completion task, the children were given one practice item to introduce them to the requirements of the sentence completion technique. This item was based on a pair of pictures from the Intentional experiment, and the sentence fragment ended with *and*. For each test item, after the experimenter had presented and described the two pictures, she read out a sentence fragment and asked the children to complete it. For empirical items, the sentence fragment was of the form *B because* ..., and for deductive items it was of the form *We can tell that B because*... For example, the sentence fragments corresponding to the questions in (6.33) and (6.34) were:

(6.35) *John has a broken leg because*... and:

(6.36) *We can tell that John has a broken leg because*...

After the children had completed the sentence, they were asked to say the whole sentence by themselves.

All the children were tested individually in a small room in their school. The child was seated beside the experimenter in front of a table. Each child received the two sessions on different days. At the beginning of the second session the child was told that the pictures would be 'a little bit' different. The sessions were recorded on audio-tape and the children's basic responses were also recorded manually.

The adult subjects received written versions of the tasks. They were presented with written descriptions of the pictures which had been shown to the children, and with written versions of the questions or sentence fragments. All the adults had also completed a questionnaire based on the Intentional experiment. The assignment of subjects to the questions and sentence completion conditions was the same for both experiments. Both questionnaires were presented to the subjects in a single booklet, and the Intentional questionnaire always preceded the Deductive/Empirical questionnaire in the booklet.

The adults who completed the acceptability judgement questionnaire did not complete any of the other questionnaires. They were presented with the written descriptions of the pictures which the children had been shown, and they were also given a brief description of the sentence completion task. Then, for each item, they were asked to rank the four sentences for acceptability using a scale which ranged from 1 ('most acceptable'/'sounds best') to 4 ('least acceptable'/'sounds worst'). Equal ranks could be assigned to sentences which the subject thought were equally acceptable. The subjects were also asked to mark (with an asterisk) any sentence which they thought was totally unacceptable. (See Appendix 5.) The four sentences which were based on the item used to illustrate the other tasks were as follows:

(6.37) *John has a broken leg because he fell off his bike.*
(6.38) *John has a broken leg because his leg is in plaster.*
(6.39) *We can tell that John has a broken leg because his leg is in plaster.*
(6.40) *We can tell that John has a broken leg because he fell off his bike.*

6.4 Results

6.4.1 *Adults' treatment of the deductive/empirical distinction*

Table 28 shows the percentage of the adults' responses to the questions and sentence completion task which were consistent with the predicted distinction between the deductive and empirical modes. These results indicate that, on the whole, the adults did draw a clear distinction between the two modes. The largest number of 'errors' occurred for the deductive items in the questions task. However, out of the 24 errors on these items, 15 were 'double' responses in which the subject referred to both element A and element C. For example, in response to *How do you know the pillow burst?*, one subject wrote:

Because Mary hit John with it and now there are feathers everywhere.

It may indeed be reasonable to say that a deduction about B draws on knowledge of the relation between A and B as well as on knowledge of the relation between B and C. Therefore, these double responses serve as an important indication that the deductive/empirical distinction is not totally clear-cut. Nevertheless, the fact that even for the deductive questions 85% of the responses did refer to element C alone is strong evidence that adults are capable of making the deductive/empirical distinction in response to linguistic cues.

In the acceptability judgement questionnaire, another group of adults was asked to judge the relative and absolute acceptability of four types of sentence:

  (i) *B because A* sentences, which correspond to 'correct' completions of empirical items. These will be referred to as 'E+' sentences.
 (ii) *We can tell that B because C* sentences, which correspond to 'correct' completions of deductive items. These will be referred to as 'D+' sentences.
(iii) *B because C* sentences, which correspond to 'incorrect' completions of empirical items. These will be referred to as 'E−' sentences.
 (iv) *We can tell that B because A* sentences, which correspond to 'incorrect' completions of deductive items. These will be referred to as 'D−' sentences.

Results

Table 28. *Percentage of adults' responses which were consistent with the deductive/empirical distinction in Experiment 6*

	Empirical items	Deductive items	Total
Questions	97.50	85.00	91.25
Sentence completion	91.25	92.50	91.88

The percentages are calculated on the basis of the total number of responses per cell.

Table 29. *Results of acceptability judgement questionnaire based on Experiment 6*

Sentence type	Sum of ranks	'Totally unacceptable'	
		f	%
B because A (E+)	377	0	0
B because C (E−)	857.5	80	31.25
We can tell that B because C (D+)	507.5	2	0.78
We can tell that B because A (D−)	818	53	20.70

Sum of ranks (across all subjects and all items); and number of judgements of 'totally unacceptable' (as frequencies and as percentages of total number of responses to each sentence type).

A measure of the relative acceptability of each sentence type was obtained by summing the ranks assigned to all the items of a given type across all the subjects. As Table 29 shows, the results are consistent with the results of the questions and sentence completion tasks, in that the E+ and D+ sentences were judged to be more acceptable than the E− and D− sentences. (Low ranks correspond to high acceptability.)

Table 29 also shows the frequency with which instances of each sentence type were judged to be 'totally unacceptable'. The pattern of these absolute judgements is consistent with the pattern obtained from the judgements of relative acceptability, in that the highest frequency of 'totally unacceptable' judgements was for E− sentences and the next highest was for D− sentences. However, the results for the judgements of absolute acceptability do not provide a clear answer to the question of whether adults actually regard E− and D− sentences as unacceptable, or whether they simply prefer the E+ and D+ versions but think all the sentence types are acceptable. Out of the 16 subjects, 8 judged at least one of the E− sentences to be totally unacceptable, and 6 judged at least one of the D− sentences to be totally unacceptable. None of the subjects judged all the sentences of a given type

Table 30. *Mean scores for each age group on each task in Experiment 6*

	Empirical items (Maximum = 16)	Deductive items (Maximum = 16)	Total (Maximum = 32)
Questions			
5 years	15.25	3.50	18.75
8 years	15.38	8.12	23.50
10 years	15.19	10.31	25.50
Sentence completion			
5 years	13.50	7.19	20.69
8 years	13.38	8.06	21.44
10 years	14.19	11.75	25.94

Table 31. *Correct responses as percentage of total number of responses per cell (Experiment 6)*

	Empirical items	Deductive items	Total
Questions			
5 years	95.31	21.88	58.59
8 years	96.09	50.78	73.44
10 years	94.92	64.45	79.69
Adults	97.50	85.00	91.25
Sentence completion			
5 years	84.38	44.92	64.65
8 years	83.59	50.39	66.99
10 years	88.67	73.44	81.05
Adults	91.25	92.50	91.88

to be totally unacceptable. Thus, there was a lack of consensus both across items and across subjects regarding the status of the E− and D− sentences.

When we consider the children's performance in this experiment, it will be worthwhile bearing in mind that, while the adult data provide some justification for classing E− and D− responses as 'incorrect', they also suggest that the distinction between 'correct' and 'incorrect' may be relative rather than absolute.

6.4.2 *Children's ability to make the deductive/empirical distinction*

Table 30 shows the mean number of items correct for each age group for the empirical and deductive items separately and for all the items combined. In Table 31 the results are presented as percentages to allow the children's performance to be compared with the adults'. The results indicate that, on

Table 32. *Number of subjects who passed (i.e. scored 12/16 or more)*
on empirical items only, deductive items only, both types of item, or neither
type of item

	Empirical only	Deductive only	Both	Neither
Questions				
5 years	15	0	1	0
8 years	11	0	5	0
10 years	8	1	7	0
Sentence completion				
5 years	9	2	3	2
8 years	7	3	5	1
10 years	5	1	10	0

Maximum per cell = 16.

Table 33. *Number of subjects assigned to systematic error category*
(i.e. who scored 4/16 or less) for empirical items compared to deductive items
in Experiment 6

	Empirical	Deductive
Questions		
5 years	0	12
8 years	0	6
10 years	0	3
Sentence completion		
5 years	0	6
8 years	0	7
10 years	1	1

the whole, the children performed very well on the empirical items, but that
they had some difficulty with the deductive items. This was explored further
by looking at the number of subjects passing each type of item. In order to
pass, a subject had to give the correct response to at least 12 out of the 16
items. (From the binomial distribution, the probability of this outcome
occurring by chance is less then 0.05.) The results in Table 32 indicate that
a considerable proportion of the subjects, especially in the younger groups,
passed only on the empirical items. The subjects who failed on the deductive
items might have done so either by responding randomly to these items or
by systematically responding to the deductive items as if they were empirical
items. A subject was assigned to the 'systematic error' category if she scored
4 or less on a particular type of item. Table 33 shows that many of the subjects

in the two younger groups tended to treat the deductive items as if they were empirical items, whereas there was almost no evidence of the opposite tendency.

6.4.3 *Age effects*

Kruskal-Wallis one-way ANOVAs indicated that there were no significant age effects for performance on the empirical items in either the questions task or the sentence completion task. On the other hand, for the deductive items, there was a significant age effect both in the questions task ($p < 0.02$) and in the sentence completion task ($p < 0.05$). Mann-Whitney U tests (1-tailed) yielded significant results for the difference between the 5-year-olds' and the 8-year-olds' performance on the deductive items in the questions task ($p < 0.025$), and for the difference between the 8-year-olds' and the 10-year-olds' performance on the deductive items in the sentence completion task ($p < 0.05$), but the other differences were non-significant. Thus, the results provide some support for the hypothesis that the ability to distinguish between the deductive and empirical modes increases with age.

6.4.4 *Temporal order and content*

It was predicted that, if the children were following an order-of-mention strategy, they would respond correctly to deductive items and incorrectly to empirical items when the underlying events/states were sequential, but that they would respond randomly to both deductive and empirical items when the underlying events/states were simultaneous. As Table 34 shows, the results fail to support this prediction, in that the pattern of results is the same for both the sequential and the simultaneous items. In both cases, performance was better for the empirical items than for the deductive items. These results indicate that the children were not making use of an order-of-mention strategy, and also that the temporal order variable did not have any effect on their performance.

The results in Table 35 indicate that performance was not affected by whether the content was physical or psychological. This is congruent with the findings of Experiments 1 to 5.

6.4.5 *Comparison between questions and sentence completion tasks*

Since the sentence fragments used in the sentence completion task are potentially ambiguous, it was predicted that the children would be better at distinguishing between the empirical and deductive modes in the questions task than in the sentence completion task. Mann-Whitney U tests (1-tailed)

Table 34. *Comparison of sequential and simultaneous items with respect to mean scores for empirical and deductive items*

	Sequential		Simultaneous	
	Empirical	Deductive	Empirical	Deductive
Questions				
5 years	7.75	1.50	7.50	2.00
8 years	7.94	3.94	7.44	4.19
10 years	7.69	5.06	7.50	5.25
Sentence completion				
5 years	6.68	3.56	6.81	3.62
8 years	6.50	4.44	6.88	3.62
10 years	7.00	6.56	7.19	5.19

Maximum per cell = 8.

Table 35. *Comparison of physical and psychological items with respect to total mean scores*

	Physical	Psychological
Questions		
5 years	9.75	9.00
8 years	11.56	11.94
10 years	12.50	13.00
Sentence completion		
5 years	10.44	10.25
8 years	10.81	10.62
10 years	13.12	12.81

Maximum per cell = 16.

showed that for the empirical items performance on the questions task was significantly better ($p < 0.025$) than performance on the sentence completion task for the 5-year-olds and for the 8-year-olds, but not for the 10-year-olds. However, for the deductive items and for the total set of items, there were no significant differences between the two tasks. Thus, there is some evidence that 5-year-olds and 8-year-olds find *Why?* more useful than *because* as a cue for them to supply a cause rather than evidence.

Since many of the issues raised by the results of this experiment are also relevant to Experiment 7, further discussion of the results will be postponed until the end of the chapter. (See section 6.8.)

6.5 Experiment 7: The Deductive Marking experiment – hypotheses

This experiment was designed to investigate the extent to which subjects would show an understanding of the deductive/empirical distinction through their use of deductive markers and of the causal connectives, when they were cued into the deductive mode by the context. It was predicted that the use of deductive markers to indicate that a conclusion was being expressed would increase with age. However, the linguistic analysis presented in section 6.1.2 implies that even adults do not regard deductive markers as obligatory and so will not always mark deductive sentences as deductive. Experiment 7 provided a test for this hypothesis. It was also predicted that the ability to use *because* and *so* in the way appropriate to the deductive mode (i.e. to follow *because* with a reference to the evidence and *so* with a reference to the conclusion) would increase with age.

The items used in this experiment varied in terms of whether the underlying events/states were simultaneous or sequential, and also in terms of whether the content was physical, psychological or logical. It seemed possible that these differences would have some effect on the way the subjects expressed their deductive explanations, though there were no grounds for formulating specific predictions.

6.6 Method

6.6.1 *Subjects*

There were 36 children in each of three age groups: 5-year-olds, 8-year-olds and 10-year-olds. The mean ages for these groups were 5;4, 8;6 and 10;4. The ages ranged from 4;11 to 5;11, from 7;11 to 8;10, and from 9;11 to 11;3. There were 18 boys and 18 girls in the 5-year-old group, 13 boys and 23 girls in the 8-year-old group, and 20 boys and 16 girls in the 10-year-old group. The children in the two older groups were attending a local authority school in Edinburgh, Wardie Primary. The 5-year-olds were tested at a later date and were attending a local authority school in Plymouth, Stoke Damerel Primary. The two schools were broadly similar with respect to the social backgrounds of their pupils.

A total of 49 undergraduates also took part in the experiment. Of these, 34 received written versions of the tasks presented to the children, and 15 completed a questionnaire which asked for judgements of the acceptability of sentences. None of the adult subjects had completed any of the other questionnaires.

6.6.2 *Design*

Half of the children in each age group received a sentence completion task, and half received an open-ended task. In the sentence completion task, the child was asked to complete sentence fragments which ended with *so*. Each sentence fragment referred to a piece of evidence which the child was expected to be able to use to draw a conclusion. In this task, the linguistic and non-linguistic contexts were such that the child would be likely to complete the sentence by referring to a conclusion. The aim of this task was to assess the extent to which the children used deductive markers to make it explicit that they were expressing a conclusion. In the open-ended task, the children were asked to report the evidence and the conclusion to an 'accomplice', but no restrictions were imposed regarding the type of linguistic construction they should use. This task was designed to provide data not only on the children's use of deductive markers, but also on their use of causal connectives.

Each task was made up of three sub-tasks, and each sub-task consisted of four items. Sub-task A involved making inferences about events which were prior to the evidence. Thus, the items in this sub-task corresponded to the items in the sequential category in the Deductive/Empirical experiment. However, for all the items in sub-task A the relation between the events/states was a physical one. Sub-task B involved making inferences about states which were simultaneous with the evidence. For two of the items the relation between the states was one of physical causality, and for the other two items it was one of psychological causality. These four items corresponded to the simultaneous items in the Deductive/Empirical experiment. Sub-task C, like sub-task B, involved making inferences about states which were simultaneous with the evidence. However, in sub-task C, the relation between the states was based on an arbitrary rule rather than being causal. This sub-task was expected to elicit deductive sentences with logical content. Each subject received all three sub-tasks in a single session. The order of the sub-tasks was counter-balanced across subjects for each age group and for each task (sentence completion or open-ended.) The order of the items within each sub-task was the same for all the subjects. (See Appendix 6.)

One group of adults (consisting of 18 subjects) received a written version of the sentence completion task, and another group (of 16 adults) received a written version of the open-ended task. For both tasks, all the adults received the sub-tasks in the same order: A, B, C. The remaining 15 adults completed a questionnaire which asked them to judge the acceptability of sentences. For each item, there were six sentences to be judged, and these sentences had the following forms:

(6.41) *B so we can tell that A.*
(6.42) *B so A (must).*
(6.43) *B so A.*
(6.44) *We can tell that A because B.*
(6.45) *A (must) because B.*
(6.46) *A because B,*

where B corresponds to the evidence and A corresponds to the conclusion. This set of sentences incorporates a number of contrasts: between explicitly deductive ((41), (42), (44), (45)) and implicitly deductive sentences ((43) and (46)); between the two different deductive markers (*can tell* and *must*); and between *so* sentences and *because* sentences. The questionnaire consisted of 12 items and these were based on the 12 items used in the sentence completion and open-ended tasks. The order of the items was the same as for the other two adult groups. The order of the six types of sentence was varied randomly across items, but was the same for all the subjects.

6.6.3 *Procedure used with children*

All the children were tested individually in a room in their school. The experimenter and the child sat at adjacent sides of a small table. All the sessions were recorded on to audio-tape.

The experiment was presented as a 'detective game' in which the child was asked to help the Pink Panther to solve some mysteries. The experimenter showed the child a toy Pink Panther, and suggested that the child try to help the Pink Panther to work out some things. Then the experimenter placed the Pink Panther behind a screen, and said to the child:

Let's pretend that the Pink Panther is in another room. The Pink Panther can't see you, but you can talk to him on the phone. I've got some clues that will help us to solve the mysteries. You have to phone the Pink Panther and tell him about the clue and about what you've worked out.

A toy phone was placed beside the Pink Panther, and another toy phone was placed on the table in front of the child. In both the sentence completion and the open-ended conditions, each clue was presented to the child non-verbally and then verbally.

In both conditions, the session began with a practice item which was used to introduce the child to the general procedure. The child was presented with the picture of John with his leg in plaster (which had been used in the Deductive/Empirical experiment), and was asked to help the Pink Panther to work out what was wrong with John.

Method

Sub-task A (sequential): The child was presented with a set of four pictures each showing a cloaked and hooded figure committing a crime. The four pictures were arranged in a row on the table, and remained there throughout the sub-task. The experimenter pointed to each picture in turn and briefly described each crime:

In this picture, someone is stealing flowers out of a garden. In this picture, someone is eating a cake. In this picture, someone is breaking into a jeweller's shop. In this picture, someone is painting red spots on to a fence.

The child was asked what was happening in each of the pictures. Then the experimenter told the child that the Pink Panther had caught the four baddies, and that the baddies were: Snoopy, Charlie Brown, Donald Duck and Mickey Mouse, but that the Pink Panther did not know 'which baddy did which naughty thing'. The child was asked to help the Pink Panther to work out what each baddy had done. For each item the child was presented with a clue which consisted of a picture of one of the four cartoon characters bearing traces of the crime which he had committed. The first picture showed Snoopy with cream on his face, the second showed Charlie Brown with red paint on his hands, the third showed Donald Duck with muddy feet, and the fourth showed Mickey Mouse with a necklace sticking out of his pocket. For each item in the sentence completion condition, the child was asked to complete a sentence fragment, such as:

> *Snoopy has cream on his face so...*

For each item in the open-ended condition, the experimenter gave a description of the clue, such as:

> *The clue is that Snoopy has cream on his face,*

and asked the child to tell the Pink Panther about the clue and about what she had worked out. (The complete set of descriptions and sentence fragments is presented in Appendix 6.) The pictures representing the clues were presented one at a time, and each picture was removed after the child had given a response.

Sub-task B (simultaneous and causal: The first two items involved deducing a person's location on the basis of physical cues. The child was told that the Pink Panther was looking for Charlie Brown and that he knew Charlie Brown always hid in houses. The child was asked to help the Pink Panther to work out which house Charlie was in. For each item the clue consisted of a picture of two houses of different colours. The picture for the first item showed a blue

125

house with footprints leading up to the door, and a yellow house with no footprints. The verbal versions of the clue were:

> *There are footprints to the blue house so...*
> *The clue is that there are footprints to the blue house.*

For the second item, the picture showed a red house with a light on in one of the rooms and a green house with no lights on. The clue was presented verbally in one of the following ways:

> *There is light on in the red house so...*
> *The clue is that there is a light on in the red house.*

The other two items in sub-task B were based on psychological rather than physical relations. The children's task was to work out how Charlie Brown was feeling on the basis of his facial expression. The children were told that the Pink Panther wanted to know whether Charlie was feeling happy, sad, cross or scared, and they were asked to help the Pink Panther to work out how Charlie was feeling. The verbal versions of these items were:

> *Charlie is crying so...*
> *The clue is that Charlie is crying.*
> *Charlie is smiling so...*
> *The clue is that Charlie is smiling,*

and the non-verbal versions were a picture of Charlie crying and a picture of Charlie smiling.

Sub-task C (simultaneous and arbitrary/logical): This consisted of two phases. In the first phase, the child was taught two biconditional rules. The experimenter placed three red tins and three green tins on the table. Each red tin contained a toy horse, and each green tin contained a toy pig. The child was asked to open all the red tins, and then all the green tins, and to say what was inside them. Then the experimenter stated the biconditional rules in the following way:

All the red tins have horses inside, haven't they?...And all the horses are in red tins, aren't they?...All the green tins have pigs inside, haven't they?...And all the pigs are in green tins, aren't they?

Next, the experimenter removed the animals from the tins, shuffled the tins, and asked the child to put the animals into the right tins. As a final check that the child had grasped the rules, the experimenter asked four questions:

> *Which tins do the pigs go into?*
> *Which animals go into the red tins?*

> *Which tins do the horses go into?*
> *Which animals go into the green tins?*

Any errors which were made either in responding to these questions or in putting the animals into the tins were corrected by the experimenter.

In the second phase of the task, the child had to use the biconditional rules as a basis for some deductions. The child was told that the Pink Panther wanted to know what was inside a tin, but that the tin was stuck shut. As a clue, the child received an envelope containing a red tin, and was asked to put the tin on the table. Then the experimenter gave the verbal version of the clue:

> *It's a red tin so...*, or
> *The clue is that it's a red tin.*

For the next item, this procedure was repeated with a green tin serving as the clue. The other two items in this sub-task required the child to deduce the colour of a hidden tin. The experimenter produced a cloth bag, and told the child that there was a tin inside it. The child was asked to help the Pink Panther to work out what colour the tin was. However, certain constraints were imposed, and the experimenter presented these to the child in the following way:

We're not allowed to look inside the special bag, and we're not allowed to take the tin out of its special bag. But I'm allowed to put my hand in and bring the animal out of the tin.

The non-verbal presentation of the clue, for these two items, consisted of the experimenter showing the animal to the child. (These were the only items for which the clue was not presented in an envelope.) For the first of these items, the animal was a horse, and for the second it was a pig. The clues were presented verbally as:

> *There's a horse/pig inside so...*
> *The clue is that there's a horse/pig inside.*

6.6.4 *Procedure used with adults*

All the adult subjects were presented with written descriptions of the contexts and clues, and were asked to read about the appropriate context and clue before completing each item. In the sentence completion condition, the subjects were asked to complete the sentence fragments in a way which would help the Pink Panther. For each item in the open-ended condition, the subjects were asked to write down what they would say if they were telling the Pink Panther about the clue and about what they had worked out. The subjects who received the acceptability judgement questionnaire were asked to assume that the sentences which they were judging were being used to tell the Pink Panther about the clue and about what had been worked out on the basis of the clue. For each item the subjects were asked to rank the six sentences for acceptability using a scale which ranged from 1 ('most acceptable'/'sounds best') to 6 ('least acceptable'/'sounds worst'). Equal ranks could be assigned to sentences which the subject thought were equally acceptable. The subjects were also asked to mark (with an asterisk) any sentence which they thought was totally unacceptable. The format and instructions were comparable to those in the questionnaire presented in Appendix 5. Here is an example of a set of six sentences based on one of the items presented to the children:

> *Snoopy has cream on his face so we can tell that he ate the cake.*
> *Snoopy has cream on his face so he must have eaten the cake.*
> *Snoopy has cream on his face so he ate the cake.*
> *We can tell that Snoopy ate the cake because he has cream on his face.*
> *Snoopy must have eaten the cake because he has cream on his face.*
> *Snoopy ate the cake because he has cream on his face.*

6.7 Results

6.7.1 *Adults' treatment of the marked/unmarked distinction*

The percentage of the adults' responses which contained deductive markers was 41.2% in the sentence completion condition and 37.5% in the open-ended condition. Thus, more than half of the responses were not marked. Also, there were 6 (out of 34) subjects who did not give any marked responses.

Table 36 shows the sum of the ranks assigned to each type of sentence in the acceptability judgement questionnaire. The results are similar to those obtained for Experiment 6, in that the sentences containing deductive markers tended to be judged as more acceptable than the unmarked sentences. The same pattern emerged when the response profiles of the individual subjects were examined. With one exception in each case, the subjects judged *B so we can tell that A* sentences to be more acceptable than *B so A* sentences, and *We can tell that A because B* sentences to be more acceptable than *A because B* sentences.

The second column in Table 36 shows the number of judgements of 'totally unacceptable' which were given for each sentence type. These judgements of absolute acceptability are broadly consistent with the judgements of relative acceptability, in that the highest number of 'totally unacceptable' judgements occurred for the *A because B* sentences. Six of the subjects said that at least one of these sentences was 'totally unacceptable', compared with

Table 36. *Results of acceptability questionnaire based on Experiment 7*

Sentence type	Sum of ranks	'Totally unacceptable'	
		f	%
B so we can tell that A	547	0	0
B so A (must)	442	0	0
B so A	796.5	4	2.22
We can tell that A because B	551	1	0.55
A (must) because B	526.5	6	3.33
A because B	917	32	17.78

Sum of ranks (across all subjects and all items); and number of judgements of 'totally unacceptable' (as frequencies and as percentages of total number of responses to each sentence type).

Table 37. *The percentage of responses for each age group which contained deductive markers, and the number of subjects who used at least one deductive marker in the sentence completion condition of Experiment 7*

	Marked responses (%)	Number of Ss
5 years ($N = 18$)	12.96	6
8 years ($N = 18$)	24.07	9
10 years ($N = 18$)	27.31	10
Adults ($N = 18$)	41.20	15

two subjects for the *B so A* sentences and one subject for the *We can tell that A because B* and the *Must A because B* sentences. However, only one subject judged all the *A because B* sentences to be 'totally unacceptable'. Furthermore, the 32 judgements of 'totally unacceptable' which were given for *A because B* sentences represent only 18% of the total number of responses for that sentence type. Thus, even the least acceptable of the sentence types is not consistently judged to be 'totally unacceptable'.

6.7.2 *Use of deductive markers*

Table 37 shows the percentage of responses which contained a deductive marker, and the number of subjects who used at least one deductive marker in the sentence completion condition.[4] (Phrases like *the one who* and *that's where* were counted as deductive markers, since they seem to indicate that a conclusion is being expressed by emphasising the fact that the speaker has made a choice from a set of alternatives.) The results indicate that the 5-year-old group used deductive markers less frequently than the other age groups, and that

Table 38. *The percentage of responses for each age group which contained deductive markers, and the number of subjects who used at least one deductive marker in the open-ended condition of Experiment 7*

	Marked responses (%)	Number of Ss
5 years ($N = 18$)	17.59	10
8 years ($N = 18$)	48.61	13
10 years ($N = 18$)	69.44	17
Adults ($N = 16$)	37.50	13

the adults used deductive markers more frequently than the children. The 8-year-old and 10-year-old groups were similar in the extent to which they used deductive markers.

Table 38 shows that, in the open-ended condition, the 5-year-old group again used deductive markers less frequently than the other age groups. However, the frequency of deductive markers was less for the adults than for the 8-year-olds and 10-year-olds. The 10-year-olds used deductive markers more frequently than any of the other age groups.

When the results for the two conditions are combined, the percentages of marked responses are: 15.28% for the 5-year-olds, 36.34% for the 8-year-olds, 48.38% for the 10-year-olds, and 39.46% for the adults. Thus, the main difference lies between the 5-year-olds and the other groups.

6.7.3 *Use of the causal connectives*

If the subjects in the open-ended condition are using the causal connectives in the way which is appropriate for the deductive mode, then they will use *because* when they mention the conclusion before the evidence (conclusion → evidence) and *so* when they mention the evidence before the conclusion (evidence → conclusion). The results presented in Table 39 indicate that all the 8-year-olds' and 10-year-olds' uses of the connectives and most of the adults' uses of the connectives conformed to this pattern. The 5-year-olds' responses included five which were inappropriate to the deductive mode, but it is difficult to interpret this finding since the 5-year-olds produced very few causal connectives overall. The percentage of the responses to the open-ended task which contained a causal connective was 12% for the 5-year-olds, 41% for the 8-year-olds, 45% for the 10-year-olds, and 46% for the adults. Thus, causal connectives were not used particularly frequently by any of the age groups, but they were used even less frequently by the 5-year-olds than by the other age groups. These results suggest that the ability to use the connectives in a way appropriate to the deductive mode *may* improve between

Table 39. *Relation between clause order and choice of connective (frequencies) in open-ended condition of Experiment 7*

	Evidence → conclusion	Conclusion → evidence
Because		
5 years	5	7
8 years	0	34
10 years	0	33
Adults	4	48
So		
5 years	14	0
8 years	55	0
10 years	64	0
Adults	36	0

the ages of 5 and 8 years. However, this conclusion must be a very tentative one: the fact that the 5-year-olds only rarely used the connectives does not necessarily indicate that they were incapable of using the connectives appropriately.

6.7.4 *Temporal order and content*

Neither the temporal order nor the content variable had any clear effect on the subjects' use of deductive markers. Also, since the causal connectives were almost always used correctly, the temporal order and content variables obviously did not affect the subjects' ability to use the connectives in the way appropriate to the deductive mode.

6.8 Discussion of Experiments 6 and 7

The experiments reported in this chapter aimed to assess the status of the empirical/deductive distinction for both children and adults, and also to investigate the use of causal connectives in the deductive mode. Experiment 6 assessed the subjects' ability to respond to the linguistic cues which can be used to signal the distinction between the modes. Experiment 7 investigated the extent to which the subjects used deductive markers to make the empirical/deductive distinction explicit, and the extent to which the subjects took account of the empirical/deductive distinction in their use of the causal connectives.

The results for the adult subjects indicate that, while a distinction can be drawn between the type of linguistic construction which is characteristic of the empirical mode and the type of linguistic construction which is characteristic of the deductive mode, the distinction is not totally clear-cut. In Experiment 7, (the Deductive Marking experiment), the adults' judgements of relative acceptability revealed a strong preference for the sentences containing deductive markers over the unmarked sentences. However, on the whole, the adults were reluctant to judge the unmarked sentences to be 'totally unacceptable'. Also, the adults who received the sentence completion and open-ended tasks produced unmarked sentences more frequently than marked sentences. Similarly, in Experiment 6 (the Deductive/Empirical experiment), the adults demonstrated an ability to make a clear distinction between deductive and empirical sentences in the questions and sentence completion tasks and when they were judging the relative acceptability of sentences. However, there was a lack of consensus (both across subjects and across items) as to whether the E— and D— sentences were 'totally unacceptable'.

These results have important implications for the way in which inversions are identified in studies of children's knowledge of *because* and *so*. Since the adults made considerable use of unmarked *because* and *so* sentences in deductive contexts and did not consistently judge such sentences to be 'totally unacceptable', it would be inappropriate to assume that sentences of the form *A because B* or *B so A* are necessarily inversions of empirical sentences. Piaget (1926,1928) claims that when young children produce such sentences they are producing inversions, and that they do so because they lack an understanding of the directional nature of causal relations. Piaget's claim that these inversions occur frequently until the age of 7 or 8 is not supported by the results of Experiments 1 to 5. However, it may be that some of the responses which Piaget classed as inversions were actually unmarked deductive sentences.

In Experiment 7, it was predicted that the frequency of deductive markers would increase with age. This prediction was confirmed with respect to the comparison between the 5-year-old and 8-year-old groups, in that the 5-year-olds produced fewer deductive markers than the 8-year-olds. (Of course, this finding should be regarded as provisional until the study is replicated using 5-year-olds and 8-year-olds drawn from the same school.) On the other hand, the 8-year-olds' and 10-year-olds' performance was very similar to the adults' regarding the frequency of deductive markers. Although unmarked responses were frequent, the fact that many of the 8- and 10-year-olds (and even some of the 5-year-olds) did make some use of deductive markers indicates that they do have the ability to mark the deductive/empirical distinction linguistically.

Experiment 7 also aimed to test the hypothesis that there would be an increase with age in the ability to use the causal connectives in the way appropriate to the deductive mode. Again, the main difference lies between the 5-year-olds and the 8-year-olds. The 5-year-olds produced causal connectives less frequently than the 8-year-olds. Furthermore, the 5-year-olds' uses of the connectives were sometimes inappropriate to the deductive mode. However, it is difficult to assess the 5-year-olds' ability to use connectives appropriately in the deductive mode since they produced very few connectives. When the 8- and 10-year-olds used *because* and *so*, they always used them in the correct way for the deductive mode. This demonstrates that 8- and 10-year-olds know how *because* and *so* are used in the deductive mode, and that they do not confuse the deductive uses with the empirical uses.

In Experiment 6 (the Deductive/Empirical experiment) the 5-year-olds did not respond to the linguistic cues which signal the deductive/empirical distinction, and they showed a strong tendency to interpret all the items as if they were in the empirical mode. This tendency was less marked for the 8-year-olds, and decreased further between the 8-year-old and 10-year-old groups. Thus, the results provide some support for the hypothesis that there is a developmental increase in the ability to respond to the linguistic cues signalling the deductive mode. However, even in the 10-year-old group 13 (out of 32) subjects did not pass on the deductive items. Similar results were obtained by Trabasso, Stein and Johnson (1981). They found that 5-year-olds and 9-year-olds showed a tendency to respond to *How can you tell that...?* questions by referring to a cause rather than to evidence, though this tendency was less strong for the 9-year-olds than for the 5-year-olds.

Thus, the results of Experiments 6 and 7 indicate that between the ages of 5 and 10 years (and probably also after 10 years) there are developmental changes regarding the production and comprehension of deductive mode explanations. Let us now consider the nature of these developmental changes in more detail.

The 5-year-olds' performance in Experiment 7 is open to several alternative interpretations. Piaget (1926, 1928) claims that 5-year-olds do not know what it is to give a justification. He argues that justification does not begin to have an 'autonomous existence' for the child until about the age of 7 or 8. Under this interpretation, a 5-year-old's failure to use deductive markers would be attributed to lack of understanding of the deductive/empirical distinction. However, it is important to bear in mind that the difference between the 5-year-olds and the other groups in Experiment 7 was only a *relative* difference in the extent to which deductive markers were used. Some of the 5-year-olds did produce some deductive markers; and, even for adults, deductive markers were produced in only about 40% of the sentences. These results have two implications. First, at least some 5-year-olds have the ability to mark the deductive/empirical distinction linguistically, which in turn implies that they have some understanding of the distinction. Second, while use of deductive markers indicates understanding of the deductive/empirical distinction, failure to use deductive markers does not necessarily indicate lack of understanding of the deductive/empirical distinction.

An alternative interpretation of the low frequency of deductive markers produced by the 5-year-olds would be that some of the 5-year-olds have still to learn how to use these linguistic cues to signal the deductive mode. It would not be surprising if it took some time for children to learn about the uses of deductive markers, given that adults do not always produce these linguistic cues to the deductive mode.

Yet another possible interpretation would be that the context created in Experiment 7 failed to cue some of the 5-year-olds in to the deductive mode. Such an explanation could perhaps account for both the low frequency of deductive markers and the low frequency of causal connectives. In other words, the 5-year-olds may have been capable of giving deductive explanations but may not have realised that the context called for deductive explanations. The cases where the 5-year-olds used *because* inappropriately for the deductive mode might also be attributable to misinterpretation of the contextual cues. This 'contextual' hypothesis receives some preliminary support from the fact that the 3- and 4-year-olds in Experiment 3 (Game with Rules) seemed to demonstrate an ability to use *because* and *so* appropriately in the deductive mode. One interesting way to test this hypothesis would be to present children with a conflict situation in which their judgements differed from those of other children and to encourage them to resolve the conflict through discussion. Such a context appears to call for deductive explanations even more strongly than the detective game used in Experiment 7. Hence, the 'contextual' hypothesis would predict that 5-year-olds would demonstrate an ability to produce deductive explanations in the 'conflict' context. If this hypothesis were supported, then this would suggest that the developmental differences obtained in Experiment 7 arise from an increasing sensitivity to contextual signals to the deductive mode rather than arising from the acquisition of the deductive/empirical distinction.

In Experiment 6, performance on deductive items improved between the ages of 5 and 10 years, and even the 10-year-olds performed less well than the adults. However, the children's difficulty in dealing with this task is probably due to the fact that they were being required to respond to the specifically linguistic cues which can be used to make the distinction between the empirical and deductive modes explicit, rather than being due to an inability to deal with the deductive mode. It may be that children do not often have to rely on these linguistic cues, since the context may usually make it clear which explanatory mode is being employed. The deductive markers may frequently be partially redundant. Support for this proposal is provided by the finding that, in Experiment 7, both the children and the adults were inclined to omit the deductive markers from their deductive explanations.

The discrepancy between the children's performance and the adults' performance is considerably greater for the Deductive/Empirical experiment than for the Deductive Marking experiment. It may be that adults (or at any rate highly educated adults) find it easier to make a consistent distinction between the two modes when they are cued into that distinction by the structure of the task (as in the Deductive/Empirical experiment) than when the situation is less constrained (as in the Deductive Marking experiment). This proposal is consistent with the finding that, while the adults in the Deductive Marking experiment produced unmarked sentences more frequently than marked sentences, the adults who completed the acceptability judgement questionnaire showed a strong preference for the marked sentences. In contrast to the adults, the children may find it difficult to focus on the relevant linguistic cues in the Deductive/Empirical experiment and to perceive the structure of the task. Thus, the adults would benefit from the constraints of the task whereas the children would not. The fact that the adults received a written version of the task may have contributed to this effect by making the contrast between the two types of item particularly obvious to the adults.

In summary, the evidence from Experiments 6 and 7 suggests that children's knowledge of the deductive mode may be rather less secure and rather slower to develop than their knowledge of the empirical mode. However, the precise nature and extent of the difficulties children encounter in relation to the deductive mode remain to be established and would merit further study. Nevertheless, the existing evidence (from Experiment 7) indicates that, at least by the age of 8, children show an understanding of the way *because* and *so* are used in the deductive mode. Thus, they know not only that *because* may be used to introduce the cause of an event or action, but also that *because* may be used to introduce the 'cause' of a conclusion, and that this 'cause' corresponds to the evidence on which the conclusion is based.

7 General discussion

7.1 Overview

The review of previous studies of the development of the causal connectives (see Chapter 2) revealed a discrepancy between the evidence from children's spontaneous speech, which indicates that children as young as $2\frac{1}{2}$ years have an understanding of the directional element of the causal connectives' meaning, and the evidence from comprehension experiments, which suggests that such understanding is not present until the age of about 7 or 8 years. Two gaps in the existing literature were also identified. First, there was a lack of systematic studies of preschool children's production of the causal connectives in an experimental setting. Second, previous experiments had been based almost exclusively on the empirical mode. The present study aimed to reduce these two gaps in our knowledge and also to provide an explanation for the discrepancy between the spontaneous speech data and the data from comprehension experiments.

In Chapter 3, some elicited production studies were reported. These yielded data on the way 3- to 5-year-olds use the causal connectives when they are giving explanations of a range of phenomena in an experimental setting.

Chapter 4 reported an experiment which was based on the empirical mode and which was designed to test a hypothesis about the reason for the discrepancy between the two types of data: the causal direction hypothesis. This hypothesis states that children understand the directional element of the causal connectives' meaning in terms of causal direction before they understand that the causal connectives can also convey information about temporal order. The results supported this hypothesis, in that performance was better on a task which allowed the children (5-, 8- and 10-year olds) to make use of knowledge about causal direction (the causal task) than on a task which required knowledge about temporal order (the temporal task). Most previous comprehension experiments have assessed the child's understanding of causal connectives by testing the child's ability to respond to the *temporal order* information which causal connectives can convey. However, the child's production and comprehension of the causal connectives in normal discourse may be guided by knowledge about causal direction rather than about temporal order.

The remaining experiments sought to extend our picture of the child's knowledge of the causal connectives' meaning to include the intentional and deductive modes. Chapter 5 reported an experiment based on the intentional mode in which 5- and 8-year-olds were presented with information about actions and the results of these actions, and were asked to explain the actions. To give a successful intentional explanation, the children had to infer that the reason for the action was the agent's intention to achieve the result, and they also had to use a linguistic construction which was appropriate to the intentional mode.

In Chapter 6, two experiments based on the deductive mode were reported. Experiment 6 (the Deductive/Empirical experiment) assessed 5-, 8- and 10-year-olds' ability to distinguish between the deductive and empirical modes on the basis of linguistic cues provided by the experimenter. To succeed in this task, the children had to respond by referring to the cause of 'B' when they were asked *Why B?* or when they were asked to complete a sentence of the form *B because*...(empirical items), and they had to respond by referring to the evidence for 'B' when they were asked *How do you know B?* or when they were asked to complete a sentence of the form *We can tell that B because*...(deductive items). Experiment 7 (the Deductive Marking experiment) investigated the extent to which 5-, 8- and 10-year-olds use deductive markers (such as *must, know that, think*) to show that they are expressing a conclusion. In order to create a context which would be likely to encourage the production of deductive explanations, this experiment was presented as a detective game in which the evidence ('clues') and conclusions ('what you've worked out') were to be reported by the child to the Pink Panther.

Although each of the experimental chapters had a different emphasis, there were also a number of common themes which were present throughout the book. The main findings will now be summarised in relation to these themes.

7.2 Summary of findings

7.2.1 *Children's knowledge of causal relations and of the causal connectives' meaning*

Even the youngest children showed an ability to distinguish between causes and effects, and an understanding of how this distinction is encoded linguistically. The preschool children who took part in the elicited production studies produced very few cause–effect inversions. When they used causal connectives, they almost always used them correctly. Similarly, in the causal task of Experiment 4, even the 5-year-olds performed at a high level. They consistently completed the *because* sentences by referring to a cause, and some of them consistently completed the *so* sentences by referring to an effect.

The results of Experiment 5 (intentional mode) both confirm and add to our impression of how competent children are at dealing with causal expressions. Again, the inversion rate was very low, which indicates that the children's ability to produce correct *because* and *so* sentences extends to the intentional mode. The children also showed that they could infer the reason for an action on the basis of information about the result of the action. At the same time, they did not confuse the reason with the result, and they made it clear that they were giving a reason rather than a result by using an appropriate linguistic construction. They also observed the distinction which holds between *because* and $so_{(i)}$ in the intentional mode, since they followed *because* with a construction containing *was going to* or *wanted to*, whereas they followed $so_{(i)}$ with a construction containing *would* or *could*.

In the sentence completion condition of the Deductive/Empirical experiment, the children in all the age groups performed at a high level on the empirical items. This lends further support to the claim that, from an early age, children know that *because* is used to introduce a cause. However, the fact that performance on empirical items was even better in the questions condition than in the sentence completion condition suggests that *Why?* is an even more powerful cue than *because*. Some of the children also responded appropriately to the linguistic cues which indicate that a deductive explanation should be given. However, in general, performance was poorer for the deductive items than for the empirical items. Indeed, a considerable number of the 5- and 8-year-olds and a few of the 10-year-olds systematically responded to the deductive items as if they were empirical items. This may indicate that the knowledge that *because* can be used to introduce a cause becomes firmly established at an earlier age that the knowledge that *because* can be used to introduce a piece of evidence. Alternatively, it may indicate that many of the younger children are not sensitive to the linguistic cues which can be used to make the distinction between the empirical and deductive modes explicit. However, this does not necessarily mean that these children totally lack an understanding of the deductive mode.

Indeed, the results of the Deductive Marking experiment suggest that, at least by the age of 8 years, children know how *because* and *so* are used in giving deductive explanations. When the 8- and 10-year-olds in this experiment used causal connectives, they always did so in the way which is appropriate to the deductive mode. That is, they used *so* to introduce the conclusion and *because* to introduce the evidence supporting the conclusion. (The results for the 5-year-olds were more ambiguous.) It may be that children are better able to reveal their understanding of the deductive mode when the context calls for a deductive explanation than when they have to respond to the linguistic cues which signal the deductive mode.

Summary of findings

The difficulty which some of the children had in responding to the linguistic cues which signal the deductive mode becomes more comprehensible when considered in the light of the finding that, in the Deductive Marking experiment, neither the adults nor the children consistently used deductive markers when they were giving deductive explanations. This suggests that when the context makes it clear that the deductive mode is being employed, the deductive markers may be regarded as redundant and may be omitted. If many of the situations which children encounter are of this type, then they will not have much occasion to rely on the linguistic cues which signal the deductive mode.

While the adults were similar to the 8- and 10-year-olds in the extent to which they used deductive markers in the Deductive Marking experiment, the adults were much better than the children at responding to the relevant linguistic cues in the Deductive/Empirical experiment. Also, although adults frequently used unmarked forms in giving deductive explanations, they showed a clear preference for the marked forms when they were asked to rank sentences for acceptability. These results highlight the fact that different types of task tap different aspects of linguistic ability, and they suggest that one of the main differences between the children and the adults may lie in the ability to focus on the deductive markers and to use them as a source of relevant information in the Deductive/Empirical experiment.

7.2.2 Developmental effects

The results of the experiments reported in this book indicate that even the younger children have a considerable ability to use and understand causal sentences in several explanatory modes. Nevertheless, some developmental effects did emerge.

Significant age effects occurred for both tasks in Experiment 4 (empirical mode). In the temporal task, the only clear effect was for the *so* items, on which the 10-year-olds performed better than the 8-year-olds, who, in turn, performed better than the 5-year-olds. In the causal task, there was a significant improvement in performance between the 5-year-olds and the 8-year-olds for the *because* items, and between the 8-year-olds and the 10-year-olds for the *so* items. However, these various age effects give rise to different interpretations. The improvement with age in performance on the *so* items in the temporal tasks is mainly attributable to an increase in the number of children using an order-of-mention strategy, although there is also evidence to suggest that some of the 10-year-olds had overcome this strategy and were showing an understanding of the connectives' function as indicators of temporal order. The developmental effect for the *so* items in the causal task also suggests that there is a major development in children's understanding of the empirical use of *so* between the ages of 8 and 10 years. On the other hand, the developmental effect for the *because* items in the causal task seems to represent a slight increase in the consistency of the responses, rather than a dramatic increase in understanding, in that all except one of the 5-year-olds scored well above chance on the *because* items.

Similarly, in Experiment 5 (intentional), the inversion rate was very low for both age groups, so the decrease in the number of inversions which occurs between the 5-year-old and the 8-year-old group probably represents the refinement of an existing ability rather than the emergence of a new ability.

In Experiment 6 (Deductive/Empirical), significant age effects were obtained for the deductive items but not for the empirical items (on which the children were performing close to ceiling level). On the deductive items, the 10-year-olds scored higher than the 8-year-olds, who scored higher than the 5-year-olds. As a group, the 5-year-olds' performance on deductive items was below chance level, and even the 10-year-olds' performance was well below the adult level. This suggests that the ability to provide deductive explanations in response to the appropriate linguistic cues (*How do you know...?* and *We can tell that...*) undergoes considerable development both between the ages of 5 and 10 and after the age of 10. However, in addition to this general upward trend, there is a large amount of individual variation within each age group.

In Experiment 7, the Deductive Marking experiment, the 5-year-olds produced deductive markers and causal connectives less frequently than the other age groups, and a few of their uses of *because* were inappropriate to the deductive mode. However, these findings require replication since the 5-year-olds were not drawn from the same school as the older children.

Thus, the most marked developmental effects occurred for performance on *so* sentences in the empirical mode and for performance on deductive items in the Deductive/Empirical experiment.

7.2.3 *'Because' and 'so'*

In the causal task of Experiment 4, performance was better on *because* items than on *so* items (for the 5- and 8-year-olds), whereas in the temporal task performance was better on *so* items than on *because* items (for the 8- and 10-year-olds). It was argued that the superior performance on *so* in the temporal task could be explained as an artefact of the order-of-mention strategy. On the other hand, the superior performance on *because* in the causal task could not readily be explained as an artefact of the children's strategies, and it was interpreted as evidence that young children understand the meaning of *because* better than the meaning of *so*. Further evidence in support of this claim comes from the finding that, when the children (in the causal task) were asked to say the whole sentence, they substituted *because* for *so* more frequently than they substituted *so* for *because*. Also, in the elicited production studies, *because* was produced more frequently than *so*.

However, the evidence for *because* being easier than *so* is restricted to the empirical mode. In the intentional experiment, there was no difference in performance between *because* and *so* sentences, either with respect to the number of intentional responses or with respect to the inversion rate. Similarly, in the open-ended condition of the Deductive Marking experiment, the children did not show a strong preference for either connective.

7.2.4 *Temporal order and causal direction*

With regard to the child's knowledge of the causal connectives' meaning, four alternative hypotheses have been put forward either in previous studies or in the present study. (See section 2.1.4.) These can be summarised as follows:

(1) The child assumes that the order-of-mention corresponds to the order-of-occurrence of the events. Therefore, he makes no distinction between *because* and *so*, and treats them both as being equivalent to *and then*. In particular tasks, this gives the appearance that the child understands *so* but not *because*.

(2) The child does not understand the directional element of the causal connectives' meaning, although he may understand that a causal relation is involved. Therefore, he responds randomly and makes no systematic distinction between *because* and *so*.

(3) The child has an understanding of the causal connectives' function as indicators of temporal order. Therefore, he makes an appropriate distinction between *because* and *so*.

(4) The child has an understanding of the causal connectives' function as indicators of causal direction. Therefore, he makes an appropriate distinction between *because* and *so*.

The results reported in the preceding section fail to support hypothesis (1). It was only in the temporal task that the children employed an order-of-mention strategy, so it is a task-specific strategy rather than an appropriate characterisation of children's knowledge of the causal connectives' meaning. Further evidence for this conclusion comes from the results of the Deductive/ Empirical experiment. If the children had been relying on the order-of-mention strategy, then, for the sequential items, they would have given correct responses to the deductive items and incorrect responses to the empirical items, whereas for the simultaneous items they would have responded randomly. However, the results did not conform to this pattern.

The results of all the experiments reported in this book argue strongly against hypothesis (2). Even preschool children have some knowledge of the connectives' meaning.

The results of Experiment 4 (empirical) constitute evidence in support of hypothesis (4) and against hypothesis (3). Performance on the causal task was better than performance on the temporal task, and even the 5-year-olds perfomed at a high level on the causal task. In contrast, on the temporal task, even in the 10-year-old group, most of the children still did not demonstrate knowledge of the connectives' function as indicators of temporal order. Furthermore, the ability which the children showed in dealing with intentional explanations can be accounted for more readily in terms of hypothesis (4) than in terms of hypothesis (3).

Thus, the results reported in this book indicate that the child's knowledge of the causal connectives' meaning cannot be characterised adequately in terms of temporal order, but should rather be characterised in terms of causal direction.

7.2.5 *Content*

Content variables were built into all the studies. Usually, the comparison was between physical and psychological content, but the elicited production studies and the Deductive Marking experiment also included some logical content, and the Intentional experiment included a cause/condition comparison. None of these content variables affected the children's performance. This indicates that children's ability to use and understand the causal connectives is not restricted to one type of content. Also, the results of the elicited production studies demonstrate that even preschool children are able to give explanations which are appropriate to the type of phenomenon they are asked to explain, and that they do not show a strong tendency to psychologise.

In Experiment 4, the 8- and 10-year-olds in the causal task performed better on the non-reversible items than on the reversible items. This suggests that pragmatic cues influence children's understanding of causal sentences. In particular, it suggests that children have a notion of plausible cause, and that they make use of this notion in their comprehension and production of causal sentences.

7.3 Implications of the research

7.3.1 *Children's linguistic ability*

A central claim of this book is that young children are remarkably competent at using and understanding the causal connectives. The findings which I have reported contribute to our picture of children's linguistic abilities by indicating that young children know much more about the semantics of *because* and *so* than most previous research would have led us to believe. This linguistic knowledge is not restricted to particular types of content: even 3-year-olds can use causal connectives appropriately to express physical, psychological and logical relations. Furthermore, young children's knowledge of the connectives is not confined to a particular mode of explanation: they can handle explanations in the empirical mode, in the intentional mode, and (at least by the age of 8) the deductive mode.

At first sight, it may appear as if this book has dealt with children's knowledge of the meanings of only two words, *because* and *so*. However, the meanings of these two words are closely intertwined with the semantic, syntactic and pragmatic characteristics of the clauses which are linked by the connectives. I have argued that an adequate linguistic analysis of the causal connectives must take these complex inter-relationships into account, and the analysis in terms of explanatory modes aims to do just that. Equally, when we study children's knowledge of the causal connectives, we do not only learn about children's knowledge of the semantics of two isolated words. We also learn about their ability to produce and understand links between clauses. In other words, we find out something about children's knowledge of the semantic and syntactic structure of sentences. This knowledge, in turn, is an important component of the ability to produce and understand discourse. Furthermore, the study provides an illustration of how the pragmatic, semantic and syntactic aspects of children's linguistic knowledge may interact. For example, in the intentional mode the children were able to coordinate their communicative purpose (of explaining an action) with the semantic constraints imposed by the connective and with the syntactic structure of the sentence. Thus, the present findings are relevant not only to the issue of children's semantic competence but also to the much broader issue of children's communicative competence.

7.3.2 *Children's cognitive ability*

The linguistic abilities discussed in the previous section presuppose certain cognitive abilities. In particular, the children must be able to distinguish between a cause and an effect, between an action and an intention, between a conclusion and evidence, and among the various modes of explanation. The linguistic knowledge is separable from these cognitive abilities in the sense that it would be possible to possess the cognitive abilities without knowing how the various distinctions are encoded linguistically. On the other hand, it would not be possible to possess the linguistic knowledge without possessing the cognitive abilities. In other words, the cognitive abilities are prerequisites of the ability to use and understand the causal connectives appropriately. This means that when children show that they are able to comprehend and produce the causal connectives adequately as they did in this study, we can conclude that they possess certain cognitive abilities.

Thus, the present findings confirm previous findings (see section 2.2) that children as young as 3 years can distinguish between causes and effects. Previous research has also indicated that young children have a notion of 'plausible cause' which enables them to select a cause which is appropriate to a given effect. Again, this was confirmed by the present findings in that the preschool children in the elicited production studies showed the ability to distinguish among physical, psychological and logical relations and to select the type of relation which was appropriate to the phenomenon they were explaining.

In order to use the causal connectives appropriately, children must also have some specific knowledge of the particular phenomenon which they are trying to explain. If they lack such knowledge, they may confuse the cause with the effect and produce an inverted causal sentence. In the present study, an attempt was made to ensure that the children would not lack the necessary world knowledge, by selecting phenomena with which they were likely to be familiar. Under these conditions, the children showed that they were able to distinguish between causes and effects, and that they understood the meaning of the causal connectives. Therefore, if children (of similar ages) produce inversions when they are asked to explain less familiar phenomena, then this is more likely to be due to a lack of world knowledge than to an inability to distinguish between causes and effects or to a lack of understanding of the causal connectives' meaning.

7.3.3 *Relationship between cognitive and linguistic abilities.*

In section 2.2 I identified an apparent discrepancy between children's understanding of the causal connectives and their understanding of causality. Most previous research implied that children understood the cause/effect distinction for about 5 years before they understood how this distinction is encoded linguistically by the causal connectives. However, the present findings eliminate this apparent discrepancy and indicate that, in this area, young children's linguistic abilities are as impressive as their cognitive abilities. Thus, its seems that there is a considerable degree of synchrony between the development of causality and the development of the causal connectives, although the exact temporal relationship between these two aspects of development has yet to be established.

Even if this 'developmental synchrony' proved to be precise, it would be compatible with my claim that there are cognitive prerequisites for the ability to use and understand causal connectives appropriately (see section 7.3.2).

The cognitive prerequisites arise because knowledge of the causal connectives' semantics necessarily draws on conceptual knowledge about the world. For example, a child who does not have some understanding of what a cause is cannot have an adequate understanding of the meaning of *because*. In this respect, linguistic ability is dependent on cognitive ability. However, it does not follow that the cognitive development must precede the linguistic development. The only constraint is that the linguistic ability cannot develop before the cognitive ability. It would be perfectly possible for the two abilities to emerge at approximately the same time. Gopnik (1984) argues convincingly that, in some other areas of development, children work simultaneously on word meanings and on the corresponding concepts.

Although I am arguing that the linguistic developments are dependent on the cognitive developments, this should not be taken to imply that the development of the causal connectives is reducible to the development of causality. As in many areas of developmental psycholinguistics, the cognitive developments are necessary but not sufficient for the linguistic developments. The child also has to learn a great deal about the linguistic system as a system in its own right. The linguistic analyses presented throughout this book attempt to characterise what the child has to learn about the linguistic structure of causal sentences. Thus, the position which I am adopting has much in common with the weak version of the 'cognition hypothesis' (Cromer, 1978).

Furthermore, the existence of cognitive prerequisites does not preclude the possibility of linguistic development contributing to cognitive development. Although children must have some knowledge about causes in order to understand *because*, they do not need to know all there is to know about causes before they can understand *because*. Indeed, most of us would have to admit to ignorance regarding some causal phenomena, yet we would presumably claim to understand the meaning of *because*. In such cases of ignorance, we may seek an explanation of the phenomenon, and our knowledge of the meaning of *because* will probably help us to understand the explanation which we receive. Thus, both children and adults may be able to use their linguistic knowledge about the causal connectives as a tool to increase their understanding of causality.

In summary, I am arguing that the linguistic ability of understanding the causal connectives and the cognitive ability of understanding causality are interdependent (yet distinct), and that the relationship can operate in both directions.

7.3.4 *Social cognition*

One of the current 'growth areas' in developmental psychology is the study of children's social cognition, their understanding of their social world. The findings of Experiment 5 contribute to this area of research since they concern children's understanding of actions and intentions. Until recently, the only studies which explored children's knowledge of intentions were moral judgement studies. However, the problems inherent in using moral judgement tasks to assess understanding of intentions have now been well-documented (see, for example, Karniol (1978); Shultz (1980); Yuill (1984); Moran and McCullers (1984)). It is clear that relying on such tasks can often lead us to under-estimate children's knowledge of intentions. Thus, there is a need for alternative research techniques, and the technique used in Experiment 5 helps to meet this need. The results indicate that 5-year-olds can distinguish between intentions and results and can infer an intention on the basis of knowledge about the result and about the action–result relation. These findings complement Yuill's finding (1984) that 3-year-olds are able to integrate information about motives with information about outcomes when they are asked to judge a person's degree of satisfaction with particular outcomes. In addition, my findings support Stein and Trabasso's argument (1982) that intentions and results are interdependent and that children may infer one from the other.

Thus, the results of Experiment 5 contribute to our knowledge of children's social cognition by indicating that young children have a good understanding of the relationships among intentions, actions and results, and that they regard an intention as a plausible cause of a person's action. Children need a concept of intention in order to make moral judgements which conform to adult standards. Consequently, while the results of moral judgement studies may not tell us much about the child's concept of intention, the results of studies (such as this one) which assess the child's concept of intention do have implications regarding moral development.

7.3.5 *The nature of developments in the ability to explain*

It is evident, from what was said in sections 7.3.1 and 7.3.2, that there are many aspects of the ability to explain which do not show any development during the age range studied. For example, even the youngest children demonstrated an understanding of the directional element of the causal connectives' meaning, of the distinction between a cause and an effect, and of the physical/psychological/logical distinction.

However, the results of the present study indicate that three types of ability do undergo development between the ages of 5 and 10 years:

(i) the ability to make inferences about temporal order on the basis of information provided by the causal connectives

(ii) the ability to deal with causal constructions which do not conform to the natural order for giving an explanation (*so* sentences in the empirical mode)

(iii) the ability to respond to and to produce the linguistic cues which can be used to signal that an explanation is in the deductive mode.

It is noteworthy that all these abilities involve dealing with particular linguistic forms in a manner which is atypical in some respect. The causal connectives' primary function is not to convey information about temporal order, but rather to convey information about causal direction. Thus, the task of making inferences about temporal order on the basis of the causal connectives is an atypical one. Similarly, *so* sentences in the empirical mode can be regarded as atypical with respect to normal communication situations. The natural order for giving an explanation is 'what is being explained' → 'explanation'. In the empirical mode, *because* sentences conform to this order but *so* sentences do not. Therefore, it was argued that if a speaker wants to focus on the causal relation, he will be more likely to use *because* than *so*. (See section 4.1.2.) The tasks of responding to and producing the linguistic cues which can be used to signal the deductive mode are atypical in that the context frequently renders such cues redundant, and also in that these deductive markers are far from universal even in adults' deductive explanations. In Karmiloff-Smith's terms (1979), the linguistic cues are being made to carry a much heavier 'communicative burden' than they would carry in normal discourse. Thus, it seems that what children are learning to do between the ages of 5 and 10 is to exploit the full range of information which can be conveyed by the causal connectives and by the deductive markers, even when the information is non-salient.

7.3.6 *Comprehension and production*

The present findings are also relevant to the relationship between comprehension and production. In section 1.6 three possible explanations of comprehension/production discrepancies were identified and these can be summarised as follows:

1. The linguistic knowledge which guides comprehension is represented separately from the linguistic knowledge which guides production.

2. The comprehension and production processes impose differential demands on the child.

3. Comprehension studies and production studies impose differential demands on the child.

According to the first two explanations, comprehension/production discrepancies reflect genuine differences been comprehension ability and production ability. According to the third explanation, comprehension/production discrepancies are attributable to methodological factors.

The discrepancy between children's ability to use causal connectives appropriately and their poor performance in comprehension experiments involving causal connectives was attributed to methodological factors. In particular, it was argued that the type of knowledge which has typically been assessed in previous comprehension experiments differs from the type of knowledge which guides children's comprehension and production of causal connectives in normal discourse. These comprehension experiments were assessing children's knowledge of the causal connectives' function as indicators of temporal order, whereas children's comprehension and production of the causal connectives are normally guided by knowledge of the connectives' function as indicators of causal direction. This argument is a specific version of the more general argument which states that a major difference between comprehension studies and production studies is that production studies typically allow children much more control over the particular type of knowledge which they use to achieve success. Comprehension experiments reflect the investigator's assumptions about the knowledge which guides adequate comprehension and production. Therefore, if there is a mismatch between these assumptions and the type of knowledge which the children are actually employing, then they will be liable to fail the task. It is important to note that for this version of the 'methodological' explanation the difference between comprehension and production studies does not map on to a similar difference between the comprehension and production processes. In normal discourse, children have control over the particular type of knowledge which they use to guide both comprehension and production. It is only in comprehension experiments that knowledge of specific linguistic rules is directly assessed. Thus, the explanation which I have proposed for the discrepancy between the comprehension and the production of causal connectives can be regarded as being purely methodological.

Of course, it does not necessarily follow that the methodological explanation will be applicable to all comprehension/production discrepancies: it may well be that for some aspects of language development there are genuine differences between comprehension ability and production ability. The proposal that there are separate linguistic representations for comprehension and for production receives some support from studies by Connell and McReynolds (1981) and by Campbell, Macdonald and Dockrell (1982). These studies involved teaching 3- to 5-year-olds to associate nonsense syllables with unfamiliar objects or pictures. The children succeeded in this task even when they had to learn one set of word–object pairings for comprehension and a different set of pairings for production. While such evidence does not *prove* that children have separate linguistic representations for comprehension and production, it does contribute to the plausibility of a dual representation theory.

The issue of the relationship between comprehension and production merits further research and debate. As yet, there are relatively few studies which attempt to make direct comparisons between the comprehension and the production of specific words or linguistic constructions. (For examples of such studies see Chapman and Miller(1975), Winitz *et al.* (1981), Clark and Hecht (1982), and Hoenigmann-Stovall (1982). There is a need for more studies which either attempt these direct comparisons or attempt to formulate and test specific explanations of previously noted comprehension/production discrepancies. There is also a need for careful discussion and clarification of the theoretical issues. We should be wary about expecting that the comprehension/production relationship will prove to be the same for all aspects and all stages of language development. We should also be wary about expecting that a single explanation will be appropriate for all comprehension/production discrepancies. Clark and Hecht (1983: 346) advocate that differences in children's performance across tasks should be 'assumed rather than regarded as problems to be explained away'. It is true that we should no longer be surprised to discover such differences. However, attempts to describe and explain these differences should be encouraged since they are likely to enrich our understanding of language development.

7.3.7 *Explanations as a research tool*

We are now in a position to assess the validity of the assumption that explanations and justifications can be used as a research tool. (See section 1.1.) The present findings indicate that young children have a secure grasp of the rudiments of the ability to explain. In particular, they know that *Why...?* signals a request for an explanation and that *because* and *so*$_{(i)}$ are used to introduce explanations. They also know that an event should be explained by referring to its cause rather than to its effect, and that an action should be explained by referring to the agent's intention to achieve a particular result rather than by referring to the result itself.

On the other hand, while the results of the Deductive Marking experiment indicate that 8-year-olds are able to handle deductive explanations when the *context* cues them into the deductive mode, the children in the Deductive/Empirical experiment had difficulty in responding to the *linguistic* cues which can be used to signal the deductive mode. Therefore, there is reason for being cautious about using children's deductive explanations (or justifications) as a research tool unless the context contains obvious cues to indicate that an explanation in the deductive mode is required.

When children are being asked for explanations in the empirical or intentional modes, the problems involved in using their explanations as a research tool are reduced. However, we are not yet in a position to rule out totally the possiblity that children's failure may be attributable to a deficit in their ability to explain rather than to a deficit in the ability which the investigator is trying to assess. Although the abilities which I have studied are fundamental components of the ability to explain, other abilities may also be important, especially when more complex phenomena are being explained. For example, if an explanation involved a number of steps or multiple causes, the child would have to be able to express these in an appropriately structured manner.

7.3.8 *Educational implications.*

At all stages of education, pupils are frequently required to give and to understand explanations. Therefore, it is reassuring to discover that by the time children enter school they have acquired the basic 'building blocks' needed for explanation. In particular, they have a good understanding of the meanings of the causal connectives, of *Why?* questions, and of the distinction between cause and effect. Thus, when children respond to their teacher's *Why?* questions by just saying '*Cos*, this is more likely to indicate a lack of knowledge about the specific phenomenon in question (or a reluctance to supply an answer!) than to indicate a general lack of understanding about what is involved in giving an explanation. It would indeed be worrying if children did not understand *Why?* and *because* until the age of 7 or 8. These words occur very frequently in conversations with young children, so if the children really believed that *because* could introduce either a cause or an effect, they would presumably have built up an extremely muddled view of the world by the time they reached the age of 7. Fortunately, the present findings yield a much more optimistic picture of young children's knowledge.

The present findings also have implications for the design of reading materials. In the early stages of learning to read, it is important that children are not confronted with written sentences which they could not understand or produce in the spoken medium (Reid, 1983). The results of Experiment 4 indicate that, in the empirical mode, children find *because* sentences easier to handle than *so* sentences. This implies that, in their reading books, children should be introduced to *because* sentences before *so* sentences. It is interesting to note that a traditional grammatical analysis would have yielded precisely the opposite conclusion on the grounds that *because* sentences involve subordination and are therefore more complex than *so* sentences, which involve coordination. Thus, it is important to establish which constructions children actually do find easiest rather than relying on predictions from grammatical theory.

Another important educational objective is that of teaching children to write. Teachers frequently observe that inexperienced writers produce compositions which are full of 'run on' sentences, that is sentences linked with *and* regardless of the nature of the semantic link which holds between the sentences. The present findings are encouraging, since they indicate that, in their spoken language, young children can make more specific and more explicit links between sentences by using causal connectives. Further research is now needed to explore possible ways of helping children to carry over this ability from speech to writing.

The major exception to the generally promising picture of children's ability to explain concerns the deductive mode. Children seem to find it rather more difficult to explain a judgement than to explain an event or an action. In particular, they experience difficulty in responding to the linguistic cues which signal the deductive mode, such as *How do you know...?* and *We can tell that...* Requests for deductive explanations are likely to be frequent in an educational context since they provide a way of checking that pupils really understand what they are doing and are not just producing correct answers through chance, imitation, or rote learning. If young children do not understand such phrases as *How do you know?*, then they may fail to realise what is required of them in these situations, unless the teacher can use contextual cues to cue the children into the deductive mode. Again, this is an area which merits further study in order to determine the precise nature of the difficulty children encounter and consequently to identify possible remedial strategies.

7.3.9 *Mental Models*

In his book *Mental Models*, Johnson-Laird (1983) presents a theory of cognition and language comprehension which gives a central role to causes and intentions. Johnson-Laird advances three main arguments concerning the importance of causes and intentions. First, knowledge of causes and intentions plays an important role in structuring our semantic representations in that 'causation' and 'intention' function as semantic operators which are used to construct complex semantic concepts from simple semantic concepts. Second, knowledge of causal relations is crucial for the interpretation and production of discourse, since the plausibility of a discourse is dependent on the extent to which it can be interpreted within a framework of general causal knowledge. Third, Johnson-Laird argues that 'our conscious minds tend to model our world at its highest level – a world of people with intentions, a world of objects and events in causal relations' (p. 476). Thus, according to Johnson-Laird, our representations of language, our discourse processes, and our representations of the world all draw heavily on knowledge about causes and intentions. My research supports Johnson-Laird's theory by demonstrating that even young children have a good understanding of causes and intentions, and are very competent at handling explanations based on these concepts.

There are also other points of contact between my approach and that of Johnson-Laird. For example, the linguistic analyses which I have proposed for causal sentences (especially in the deductive mode) lend support to Johnson-Laird's arguments about the interdependence of intensions and reference and about the interplay between linguistic and contextual cues. Similarly, my argument that there is a two-way relationship between understanding the causal connectives and understanding causality has much in common with Johnson-Laird's view of the two-way relationship between utterances and mental models. In order to understand the meaning of the causal connectives, children must have a mental model which represents causal relations. However, as Johnson-Laird points out, a mental model can be useful even if it is neither complete nor entirely accurate. Once children have a basic knowledge of the connectives' meaning, they can presumably use this knowledge to modify or construct mental models to match their interpretations of causal sentences. Thus, the linguistic ability of understanding the causal connectives may both depend on and contribute to the cognitive ability of understanding the causal relations which structure the world.

7.3.10 *Implications for future research*

The findings of the present study suggest a number of directions which future research might take. Further investigations of children's ability to deal with explanations in the deductive mode would be likely to prove fruitful. It would be particularly worthwhile to try to identify the precise nature of the children's difficulty in distinguishing between the deductive and empirical modes in Experiment 6, and to explore ways of helping them to overcome their difficulties. Similarly, it would be interesting to explore the reasons for the low frequency of deductive markers produced by the 5-year-olds in Experiment 7. Since deductive explanations play an especially important role in the educational process, it would be useful to know more about children's strengths and weaknesses in this area.

Also, having established that young children possess the basic 'building blocks' for giving explanations, we should now ask what further developments there may be in the ability to explain. One possible type of development would be in the child's notion of plausible cause. The present study employed only content with which the children were likely to be familiar and only very simple causal chains in which each event had a single cause. Also, all the causes were facilitative rather than inhibitory, in that they made another event occur rather than preventing it from occurring. It seems likely that children's notions of plausible cause will become more and more elaborate as their knowledge of the world increases and as they begin to understand more complex causal relations such as those involving multiple or interacting causes. Research on children's causal inferences does appear to be thriving at present (Sedlak and Kurtz, 1981), but so far it has had a social or a cognitive bias. It would be interesting to introduce a more linguistic dimension by investigating the relationship between the nature of children's causal inferences and the way they express these inferences linguistically when they are giving explanations (if they do express them at all).

Another possible development concerns the role of the causal connectives. So far, I have stressed the intimate connection between knowledge of the causal connectives' meaning and the notion of plausible cause. This implies that the connective's role is usually to reinforce a causal link which is compatible with the hearer's notion of plausible cause. However, I have also argued that it is possible to use a causal connective to inform the hearer of a causal link which was outside his previous knowledge. In such a case, the communicative burden on the connective is increased, since the connective is the hearer's main evidence for assuming that the causal link exists. This way of using the connectives constitutes an extremely powerful intellectual tool, because it is a way of extending the hearer's notion of plausible cause. Therefore, it would be useful to find out when this 'autonomous' role of the connectives begins to develop.

7.3.11 *Implications for our view of the young child*

The results presented in this book create a very promising picture of the young child's knowledge of the causal connectives and of explanation. This picture is in sharp contrast to the picture which had previously been built up on the basis of Piaget's work and on the basis of comprehension experiments involving the causal connectives. (See Chapter 2.) Instead of seeing the young child as being in a state of confusion in which causes are indistinguishable from effects, physical relations are interpreted as psychological relations, and *because* lacks a clear meaning, we can now view the child's knowledge and abilities in a much more positive light. Well before the age of 7, children are able to distinguish appropriately between causes and effects, and among physical, psychological and logical relations. They also know that *because* is used to introduce a cause, and this knowledge enables them to produce well-formed causal sentences. Moreover, their ability is not restricted to explanations in the empirical mode, but extends to the intentional mode. They know that an action can be explained in terms of the agent's intention to achieve a particular result, and they are able to distinguish between the intention–

action relation and the action–result relation, and to mark the distinction linguistically.

The linguistic analyses presented in this book have revealed that the linguistic structure of causal sentences is much more complex than previous investigators had assumed it to be. Thus, it is clear that the child's task is not an easy one. However, it is also clear that the young child is equal to the task.

Appendix 1
Details of procedures for elicited production experiments

Experiment 1: Ker Plunk (physical)

The apparatus is presented without any sticks inserted, but with a bundle of sticks lying beside it.

E: Have you ever played with this toy before?...Watch what happens.

Some marbles are dropped through the hole at the top of the tube.

E: What happened?...The marbles fell down and made a loud noise, didn't they? I don't want the marbles to fall down and make a loud noise... I wonder how I could stop them falling. ...Maybe I could put these sticks in here.

The experimenter inserts the sticks (and invites the child to help).

E: What do you think will happen now?...What do you think will happen when I put the marbles in?

The experimenter drops in some marbles. (They should stay on the sticks!)

E: What happened?...Oh! I've changed my mind now. I want the marbles to fall down and make a loud noise again. ...How could I make the marbles fall?...Maybe I could pull out some sticks. ...What do you think will happen when I pull out some sticks?...

The experimenter pulls out some sticks which are not supporting any marbles.

E: What happened?...I wonder why. ...Do you know why?...

The experimenter pulls out some sticks which are supporting some marbles.

E: What happened?...I wonder why. ...Do you know why?...Now, let's see who's here.

The experimenter brings out a large toy panda from behind a screen.

E: This is Choo-Choo. Choo-Choo has not seen this toy before. Please will you play with the toy, and tell Choo-Choo all about what is happening?

Where necessary, the experimenter encourages the child to give explanations, with comments like:

> Choo-Choo wants to know what's happening.

and:

> Tell Choo-Choo why that happened.

Experiment 2: Facial Expressions (psychological)

The experimenter presents the boy/girl doll.

E: What's this?...It's a boy/girl, isn't it?...The boy/girl is called Jack/Jill. Look, we can give Jack/Jill a happy face, or a sad face, or a cross face, or a scared face.

(The experimenter attaches each face to the doll as she names it, and then removes it.)

E: Now, let's play a game. I'll put one of the faces on Jack/Jill.

The experimenter attaches one of the faces (chosen at random) to the doll.

E: Oh look, it's the happy/sad/cross/scared face. I'd like you to tell me a little story about Jack/Jill. ...What do you think has happened to Jack/Jill?...What do you think Jack/Jill has done?...I wonder why Jack/Jill is happy/sad/cross/scared. ...Why is Jack/Jill happy/sad/cross/scared?...

(This is repeated for each of the facial expressions.)

Experiment 3: Game with Rules (logical)

The materials are presented. (See Figure 3.)

E: Look what we've got here. This is a river. These are stepping-stones. There are red stepping-stones, green stepping-stones, and yellow stepping-stones. This is a piece of cheese. This is a dice with colours on it.

(The experimenter points to each item as she mentions it.)

E: Now, I'll tell you how to play the game. You move this mouse. I'll move this mouse. The mouse which gets to the cheese first will be the winner. Your mouse can only go on to these stepping-stones, and my mouse can only go on to these stepping-stones. We throw the dice and see what colour we get. The colour on the dice has to be the same as the colour of the stepping-stone for you to put your mouse on the stepping-stone. The mice must stay on the stepping-stones. They must not go into the water. The mice must jump on to all the stepping-stones. They must not miss out any stepping-stones. Now, let's try playing the game. You throw the dice first....What colour did you get?...So, what do you do?...

If the child gives a correct response, the experimenter says, 'That's right.'

If the child gives an incorrect response, the experimenter says, 'Can you do that?...No, you can't do that,' and then re-states the rule which has been violated.

E: Now, I'll throw the dice.

This procedure is continued until two games have been completed.

E: Now, let's see who's here.

The toy panda, Choo-Choo, is presented.

E: Do you remember him?...Who is this?...This is Choo-Choo. Choo-Choo would like to play the game too, but he doesn't know how to play. Please will you tell Choo-Choo how to play the game?

Where necessary, the experimenter prompts the child with comments like: 'Tell Choo-Choo what to do' and 'Is there anything else he has to do? until the child seems to have completed his explanation.

E: OK. Let's see if Choo-Choo can play the game with you now. Choo-Choo says: '[the child's name], please will you tell me if I make a mistake?' OK? You tell Choo-Choo if he does anything wrong. I'll help him to throw the dice and move his mouse.

The experimenter tries to ensure that Choo-Choo makes a couple of mistakes. If the child points out a mistake, the experimenter says 'Oh, Choo-Choo's wrong, is he?...Tell him what he's done wrong. ...Tell Choo-Choo why he's wrong?...What should Choo-Choo have done?' If the child fails to point out a mistake, then at the end of the game the experimenter asks:

> Did Choo-Choo do anything wrong?...Tell him what he did wrong. ...Tell Choo-Choo why he's wrong. ...What should Choo-Choo have done?...

Appendix 2
Sequences and items
for Experiment 4

Causal sequences

Psychological reversible

    (1) Coco pulls Daisy's hair → Daisy hits Coco → Coco pushes Daisy.
    (2) Daisy laughs at Coco → Coco gets cross → Daisy runs away.

Physical reversible

    (3) Coco bumps into Daisy → Daisy falls → Daisy has a sore leg.
    (4) The boat hits a rock → the boat tips → Mary falls out.

Psychological non-reversible

    (5) Coco breaks Daisy's doll → Daisy starts to cry → Coco gives Daisy a sweetie.
    (6) Daisy gives Coco a spider → Coco gets a fright → Daisy laughs at Coco.

Physical non-reversible

    (7) Daisy pushes Coco → Coco falls into the flowerpot → Coco gets all dirty.
    (8) Coco pushes the cup → the cup falls → the cup breaks.

Sequences and items for Experiment 4

Items for causal task

Item	Sentence	Pictures	Position	Subset
(1)a	Daisy hits Coco because...	(COCO PULLS HAIR) (COCO PUSHES DAISY)	5	A
(1)b	Daisy hits Coco so...	(COCO PULLS HAIR) (COCO PUSHES DAISY)	5	B
(2)a	Coco gets cross because...	(DAISY LAUGHS) (DAISY RUNS AWAY)	3	B
(2)b	Coco gets cross so...	(DAISY LAUGHS) (DAISY RUNS AWAY)	3	A
(3)a	Daisy falls because...	(DAISY HAS SORE LEG) (COCO BUMPS DAISY)	6	A
(3)b	Daisy falls so...	(DAISY HAS SORE LEG) (COCO BUMPS DAISY)	6	B
(4)a	The boat tips because...	(MARY FALLS OUT) (BOAT HITS ROCK)	4	B
(4)b	The boat tips so...	(MARY FALLS OUT) (BOAT HITS ROCK)	4	A
(5)a	Daisy starts to cry because...	(COCO BREAKS DOLL) (COCO GIVES SWEETIE)	1	A
(5)b	Daisy starts to cry so...	(COCO BREAKS DOLL) (COCO GIVES SWEETIE)	1	B
(6)a	Coco gets a fright because...	(DAISY GIVES SPIDER) (DAISY LAUGHS)	7	B
(6)b	Coco gets a fright so...	(DAISY GIVES SPIDER) (DAISY LAUGHS)	7	A
(7)a	Coco falls into the flowerpot because...	(COCO GETS DIRTY) (DAISY PUSHES COCO)	8	A
(7)b	Coco falls into the flowerpot so...	(COCO GETS DIRTY) (DAISY PUSHES COCO)	8	B
(8)a	The cup falls because...	(CUP BREAKS) (COCO PUSHES CUP)	2	B
(8)b	The cup falls so...	(CUP BREAKS) (COCO PUSHES CUP)	2	A

Notes: The 'Pictures' column gives descriptions of the pictures which were presented for each item, and the position of each description corresponds to the position in which the picture was placed on the table. The pictures used are reproduced in my Ph.D. thesis, 'A psycholinguistic study of children's explanations', University of Edinburgh, 1983.

The numbers in the 'Position' column refer to the position of each item in the order of presentation (e.g. item (2) was the third item to be presented in any session).

The 'Subset' column indicates which of the two parallel subsets each item was assigned to.

Items for temporal task

Item	Sentence	Picture-strips	Position	Subset
(1)a	Daisy hits Coco because he pulls her hair	(COCO PULLS HAIR → DAISY HITS)[1] (DAISY HITS → COCO PULLS HAIR)	5	A
(1)b	Daisy hits Coco so he pushes her	(COCO PUSHES DAISY → DAISY HITS) (DAISY HITS → COCO PUSHES DAISY)[1]	5	B
(2)a	Coco gets cross because Daisy laughs at him	(DAISY LAUGHS → COCO GETS CROSS) (COCO GETS CROSS → DAISY LAUGHS)[1]	3	B
(2)b	Coco gets cross so Daisy runs away	(DAISY RUNS AWAY → COCO GETS CROSS)[1] (COCO GETS CROSS → DAISY RUNS AWAY)	3	A
(3)a	Daisy falls because Coco bumps into her	(DAISY FALLS → COCO BUMPS DAISY) (COCO BUMPS DAISY → DAISY FALLS)[1]	6	A
(3)b	Daisy falls so she has a sore leg	(DAISY FALLS → DAISY HAS SORE LEG)[1] (DAISY HAS SORE LEG → DAISY FALLS)	6	B
(4)a	The boat tips because it hits a rock	(BOAT TIPS → BOAT HITS ROCK)[1] (BOAT HITS ROCK → BOAT TIPS)	4	B
(4)b	The boat tips so Mary falls out	(BOAT TIPS → MARY FALLS OUT) (MARY FALLS OUT → BOAT TIPS)[1]	4	A
(5)a	Daisy starts to cry because Coco breaks her doll	(COCO BREAKS DOLL → DAISY CRIES) (DAISY CRIES → COCO BREAKS DOLL)[1]	1	A

		Picture-strips	Position	Subset
(5)b	Daisy starts to cry so Coco gives her a sweetie	(COCO GIVES SWEETIE → DAISY CRIES)[1] (DAISY CRIES → COCO GIVES SWEETIE)	I	B
(6)a	Coco gets a fright because Daisy gives him a spider	(DAISY GIVES SPIDER → COCO GETS FRIGHT)[1] (COCO GETS FRIGHT → DAISY GIVES SPIDER)	7	B
(6)b	Coco gets a fright so Daisy laughs at him	(DAISY LAUGHS → COCO GETS FRIGHT) (COCO GETS FRIGHT → DAISY LAUGHS)[1]	7	A
(7)a	Coco falls into the flowerpot because Daisy pushes him	(COCO FALLS → DAISY PUSHES COCO)[1] (DAISY PUSHES COCO → COCO FALLS)	8	A
(7)b	Coco falls into the flowerpot so he gets all dirty	(COCO FALLS → COCO GETS DIRTY) (COCO GETS DIRTY → COCO FALLS)[1]	8	B
(8)a	The cup falls because Coco pushes it	(CUP FALLS → COCO PUSHES CUP) (COCO PUSHES CUP → CUP FALLS)[1]	2	B
(8)b	The cup falls so it breaks	(CUP FALLS → CUP BREAKS)[1] (CUP BREAKS → CUP FALLS)	2	A

Notes: The 'Picture-strips' column gives descriptions of the pictures which were presented for each item, and the position of each description corresponds to the position in which the picture-strip was placed on the table. The pictures used are reproduced in my Ph.D. thesis, 'A psycholinguistic study of children's explanations', University of Edinburgh, 1983.

The superscript [1] designates the picture-strip which was presented first for a given item.

The numbers in the 'Position' column refer to the position of each item in the order of presentation (e.g. item (2) was the third item to be presented in any session).

The 'Subset' column indicates which of the two parallel subsets each item was assigned to.

Appendix 3

Stories and items used in Experiment 5

Stories

1. Psychological cause

One day, when Mary was out shopping, she bought a silly nose. It was big, round, black, shiny nose, on a piece of elastic. When she got home, she put the nose on. Then, she said to Fluff, the cat – 'Come on, Fluff, let's go and look for John.' When John saw Mary wearing her silly nose, he laughed and laughed and laughed. He thought it was really funny. Mary was very pleased.

(ACTION = Mary put on a silly nose.
RESULT = John laughed.)

2. Distractor: physical cause

Mummy said: 'Come on, Mary. It's bath-time.' Mummy and Mary started to go upstairs. But, just then, the phone rang so Mummy went to answer the phone and Mary went up to the bathroom by herself. Mary put the plug in the bath and turned on the taps. Out came the water with a big 'Whoosh!' Soon, the bath filled up with water. Mary shouted: 'All ready, Mummy!'

(ACTION = Mary turned on the taps.
RESULT = The bath filled up with water.)

3. Physical condition

John took his Daddy's spade out of the garden shed, and he dug some holes in the garden – one, two, three holes. Then, he put a little tree into each hole. Planting trees is very hard work, so when John had finished, he went into the house and had a nice big drink of juice.

(ACTION = John dug some holes.
RESULT = John planted some trees.)

4. Psychological condition

One day, after lunch, Mary went upstairs and put on her pretty dress. Mary brushed her hair and her Mummy tied her ribbons for her. Then, Mary said goodbye to Mummy and went to Anne's house. It was Anne's birthday so she was having a party. When Anne opened the door, Mary said, 'Happy Birthday, Anne' and gave Anne a present. Then, Mary went into the party. Everybody had a lovely time.

(ACTION = Mary put on a pretty dress.
RESULT = Mary went to a party.)

5. Physical cause

Every day, John filled up his watering can with water and went out into the garden. Very carefully, he poured some water on to all the bulbs, and he tried not to stand on any of the bulbs. The bulbs grew and grew and grew, until one day there were lots of beautiful flowers in the garden.
(ACTION = John watered the bulbs.
RESULT = Flowers grew.)

6. Distractor: physical condition

One morning when Mummy was outside hanging up the washing, Mary was feeling hungry. She remembered that there was a jar of sweets on a shelf in the kitchen. She put a stool under the shelf, and, very carefully, she climbed up on to the stool. She pulled the lid off the jar, and took out some sweets. Then, she popped the sweets into her mouth.
(ACTION = Mary climbed on to a stool.
RESULT = Mary got some sweets.)

7. Psychological condition

This is Mr Jones. He has lots of lovely flowers on his little cart. One day, John bought a nice bunch of flowers from Mr Jones. Then, John walked along the road to the hospital, and went inside to visit his Granny. Granny was in hospital because she wasn't very well. Granny said – 'These are beautiful flowers, John. Thank you very much for bringing them to me.'
(ACTION = John bought a bunch of flowers.
RESULT = John visited his Granny in hospital.)

8. Physical cause

One day, John got a new toy – it was a toy car. John wound up the toy car with a special little key. Then, he put the car down on the floor and off it went – Broom, broom, broom! John said – 'This is a great toy.'
(ACTION = John wound up the car.
RESULT = The car went.)

9. Distractor: psychological condition

It was a rainy day so Mary couldn't go outside to play. She put on her nurse's outfit. It was a lovely outfit – there was a little hat, an apron, and a dress with blue and white stripes. Mary played at 'hospitals'. She put bandages on Teddy's arms and on his head. Then, she tucked him up in bed.
(ACTION = Mary put on her nurse's outfit.
RESULT = Mary played at 'hospitals'.)

10. *Physical condition*

One day, after breakfast, John put some old, stale bread into a little bag. Then, he went to the pond in the park. There were lots of ducks swimming on the pond. John broke the bread into little pieces and threw the bits of bread to the ducks. The ducks gobbled the bread up – gobble! gobble! gobble! All gone.
(ACTION = John put some bread in a bag.
RESULT = John fed the ducks.)

11. *Psychological cause*

One night, just before bed-time, John crept upstairs very, very quietly. He went into Mary's bedroom and put a little mouse in her bed. Then, John ran away and hid. Mary went into her bedroom, and picked up her cuddly rabbit. Then, she found the mouse in her bed. She screamed: 'Eee! Eee! A mouse!' Poor Mary got a terrible fright.
(ACTION = John put a mouse in Mary's bed.
RESULT = Mary got a fright.)

12. *Psychological condition*

John went into the bathroom and washed his hands. Then, he went downstairs and started eating his tea. He ate some sandwiches, and a little cake with a cherry on top, and he drank a cup of milk. The cat and the dog wanted something to eat too, but John didn't give them anything.
(ACTION = John washed his hands.
RESULT = John ate his tea.)

13. *Distractor: psychological cause*

John went into the kitchen and he saw some dirty dishes beside the sink. John put on his apron. Then, he filled the sink with warm, soapy water, and washed up all the dishes. Mummy came into the kitchen and saw that the dishes were all nice and clean. She said: 'Oh, what a lovely surprise! Thank you very much, John.'
(ACTION = John washed up all the dishes.
RESULT = Mummy got a surprise.)

14. *Physical condition*

Mary opened the drawer and took out her crayons. Then, she shut the drawer and sat down at the table. She opened her colouring book and started colouring in a picture. Her teddy was sitting on top of the chest of drawers. Maybe he was watching what Mary was doing.
(ACTION = Mary took out her crayons.
RESULT = Mary coloured in.)

15. Psychological cause

Mary put a dog biscuit down on the carpet just outside her bedroom door. She put down another biscuit, and another, and another, and another. Then, she sat down on her bed and waited. Soon, Blackie, the dog, started eating the biscuits, and he went right into Mary's room. Mary said – 'Hello, Blackie. You are a nice dog,' and she shut her bedroom door quickly. Blackie couldn't get out.
(ACTION = Mary put down some dog biscuits.
RESULT = The dog went into Mary's room.)

16. Physical cause

One day, Mary and Blackie the dog went to the train station to meet Auntie Lucy. Auntie Lucy was very tired so she sat down on a seat for a little while. Mary found a chocolate machine. She stood on her tiptoes, and put some money into the machine. Out popped a lovely big bar of chocolate!
(ACTION = Mary put some money into the machine.
RESULT = A bar of chocolate came out.)

Items used in questions task: according to age group and item set (A/B)

	5 years		8 years
	Set A	Set B	
1. Why did Mary put on a silly nose?	✓	—	✓
Mary put on a silly nose, didn't she?...			
Then what happened?	—	✓	—
2. Mary turned on the taps, didn't she?...			
Then what happened?	—	—	✓
3. Why did John dig some holes?	—	✓	✓
John dug some holes, didn't he?			
...Then what did he do?	✓	—	—
4. Why did Mary put on a pretty dress?	—	✓	✓
Mary put on a pretty dress, didn't she?...			
Then what did she do?	✓	—	—
5. Why did John water the bulbs?	—	✓	✓
John watered the bulbs, didn't he?...			
Then what happened?	✓	—	—
6. Mary climbed on to the stool, didn't she?...			
Then what did she do?	—	—	✓
7. Why did John buy a bunch of flowers?	✓	—	✓
John bought a bunch of flowers, didn't he?...			
Then what did he do?	—	✓	—
8. Why did John wind up the car?	✓	—	✓
John wound up the car, didn't he?			
...Then what happened?	—	✓	—

	5 years		8 years
	Set A	Set B	
9. Mary put on her nurse's outfit, didn't she? ...Then what did she do?	—	—	✓
10. Why did John put some bread into a bag?	✓	—	✓
John put some bread into a bag, didn't he? ...Then what did he do?	—	✓	—
11. Why did John put a mouse in Mary's bed?	—	✓	✓
John put a mouse in Mary's bed, didn't he? ...Then what happened?	✓	—	—
12. Why did John wash his hands?	—	✓	✓
John washed his hands, didn't he?...Then what did he do?	✓	—	—
13. John washed up all the dishes, didn't he? ...Then what happened?	—	—	✓
14. Why did Mary take out her crayons?	✓	—	✓
Mary took out her crayons, didn't she? ...Then what did she do?	—	✓	—
15. Why did Mary put down some dog biscuits?	✓	—	✓
Mary put down some dog biscuits, didn't she? ...Then what happened?	—	✓	—
16. Why did Mary put some money into the machine?	—	✓	✓
Mary put some money into the machine, didn't she?...Then what happened?	✓	—	—

Stories and items used in Experiment 5

Items used in sentence completion task

		Set A	Set B
1.	Mary put on a silly nose because...	✓	—
	Mary put on a silly nose so...	—	✓
2.	Mary turned on the taps and then...	✓	✓
3.	John dug some holes because...	—	✓
	John dug some holes so...	✓	—
4.	Mary put on a pretty dress because...	—	✓
	Mary put on a pretty dress so...	✓	—
5.	John watered the bulbs because...	—	✓
	John watered the bulbs so...	✓	—
6.	Mary climbed on to the stool and then...	✓	✓
7.	John bought a bunch of flowers because...	✓	—
	John bought a bunch of flowers so...	—	✓
8.	John wound up the car because...	✓	—
	John wound up the car so...	—	✓
9.	Mary put on her nurse's outfit and then...	✓	✓
10.	John put some bread into a bag because...	✓	—
	John put some bread into a bag so...	—	✓
11.	John put a mouse in Mary's bed because...	—	✓
	John put a mouse in Mary's bed so...	✓	—
12.	John washed his hands because...	—	✓
	John washed his hands so...	✓	—
13.	John washed up all the dishes and then...	✓	✓
14.	Mary took out her crayons because...	✓	—
	Mary took out her crayons so...	—	✓
15.	Mary put down some dog biscuits because...	✓	—
	Mary put down some dog biscuits so...	—	✓
16.	Mary put some money into the machine because...	—	✓
	Mary put some money into the machine so...	✓	—

Appendix 4
Materials used in Experiment 6
(Deductive/Empirical)

Sequences

Psychological + simultaneous

   1. John breaks Mary's doll → Mary is sad → Mary is crying.
   7. Mary hides John's car → John is cross → John is stamping his feet.
 11. Mary finds a mouse in her bed → Mary is scared → Mary is hiding in the corner.
 15. Mummy buys John an ice-cream → John is happy → John is smiling.

Psychological + sequential

   2. John scribbles on the wallpaper → Mummy gives John a row → John is crying.
   8. John washes up all the dishes → Mummy tells John he is a good boy → John is smiling.
 10. Mary tears John's book → John shouts at Mary → Mary has her hands over her ears.
 12. Mary paints a beautiful picture for the competition → Mary wins a prize → Mary is dancing round the room.

Physical + simultaneous

   3. John drops a match → the house is on fire → flames and smoke are coming out of the house.
   5. Mary gets soaked → Mary has a cold → Mary is sneezing.
 14. John falls of his bike → John has a broken leg → John's leg is in plaster.
 16. Mary switches on the kettle → the kettle is boiling → steam is coming out of the kettle.

Physical + sequential

   4. Mary hits John with a pillow → the pillow bursts → Mary is covered in feathers.
   6. Mary trips over the cat → Mary falls into the pond → Mary is dripping wet.
   9. John throws a ball at the window → the window breaks → there is broken glass on the ground.
 13. John bumps into Mary → Mary spills the milk → there is a puddle of milk on the floor.

Materials used in Experiment 6

Items used in questions task: subset A

(Arranged in order of presentation.)

1. Mary is sad, isn't she?...Why is Mary sad?
2. Mummy gave John a row, didn't she?...Why did Mummy give John a row?
3. The house is on fire, isn't it?...How do you know the house is on fire?
4. The pillow burst, didn't it?...Why did the pillow burst?
5. Mary has a cold, hasn't she?...Why does Mary have a cold?
6. Mary fell into the pond, didn't she?...How do you know Mary fell into the pond?
7. John is cross, isn't he?...How do you know John is cross?
8. Mummy told John he was a good boy, didn't she?...How do you know Mummy told John he was a good boy?
9. The window broke, didn't it?...How do you know the window broke?
10. John shouted at Mary, didn't he?...How do you know John shouted at Mary?
11. Mary is scared, isn't she?...Why is Mary scared?
12. Mary won a prize, didn't she?...Why did Mary win a prize?
13. Mary spilt the milk, didn't she?...Why did Mary spill the milk?
14. John has a broken leg, hasn't he?...Why does John have a broken leg?
15. John is happy, isn't he?...How do you know John is happy?
16. The kettle is boiling, isn't it?...How do you know the kettle is boiling?

Items used in questions task: subset B

1. Mary is sad, isn't she?...How do you know Mary is sad?
2. Mummy gave John a row, didn't she?...How do you know Mummy gave John a row?
3. The house is on fire, isn't it?...Why is the house on fire?
4. The pillow burst, didn't it?...How do you know the pillow burst?
5. Mary has a cold, hasn't she?...How do you know Mary has a cold?
6. Mary fell into the pond, didn't she?...Why did Mary fall into the pond?
7. John is cross, isn't he?...Why is John cross?
8. Mummy told John he was a good boy, didn't she?...Why did Mummy tell John he was a good boy?
9. The window broke, didn't it?...Why did the window break?
10. John shouted at Mary, didn't he?...Why did John shout at Mary?
11. Mary is scared, isn't she?...How do you know Mary is scared?
12. Mary won a prize, didn't she?...How do you know Mary won a prize?
13. Mary spilt the milk, didn't she?...How do you know Mary spilt the milk?
14. John has a broken leg, hasn't he?...How do you know John has a broken leg?
15. John is happy, isn't he?...Why is John happy?
16. The kettle is boiling, isn't it?...Why is the kettle boiling?

Items used in sentence completion task: subset A

1. Mary is sad because...
2. Mummy gave John a row because...
3. We can tell that the house is on fire because...
4. The pillow burst because...
5. Mary has a cold because...
6. We can tell that Mary fell into the pond because...
7. We can tell that John is cross because...
8. We can tell that Mummy told John he was a good boy because...
9. We can tell that the window broke because...
10. We can tell that John shouted at Mary because...
11. Mary is scared because...
12. Mary won a prize because...
13. Mary spilt the milk because...
14. John has a broken leg because...
15. We can tell that John is happy because....
16. We can tell that the kettle is boiling because...

Items used in sentence completion task: subset B

1. We can tell that Mary is sad because...
2. We can tell that Mummy gave John a row because...
3. The house is on fire because....
4. We can tell that the pillow burst because...
5. We can tell that Mary has a cold because...
6. Mary fell into the pond because...
7. John is cross because...
8. Mummy told John he was a good boy because...
9. The window broke because...
10. John shouted at Mary because...
11. We can tell that Mary is scared because...
12. We can tell that Mary won a prize because...
13. We can tell that Mary spilt the milk because...
14. We can tell that John has a broken leg because...
15. John is happy because...
16. The kettle is boiling because...

Descriptions of pictures (for both tasks)*

1(i) John breaks Mary's doll.
 (ii) Mary is crying.
2(i) John scribbles on the wallpaper.
 (ii) John is crying.
3(i) John drops a match.
 (ii) Flames and smoke are coming out of the house.

---

*The pictures used are reproduced in my PhD thesis, 'A psycholinguistic study of children's explanations', University of Edinburgh, 1983.

4(i) Mary hits John with a pillow.
  (ii) Mary is covered in feathers.
5(i) Mary gets soaked.
  (ii) Mary is sneezing.
6(i) Mary trips over the cat.
  (ii) Mary is dripping wet.
7(i) Mary hides John's car.
  (ii) John is stamping his feet.
8(i) John washes up all the dishes.
  (ii) John is smiling.
9(i) John throws a ball at the window.
  (ii) There is broken glass on the ground.
10(i) Mary tears John's book.
  (ii) Mary has her hands over her ears.
11(i) Mary finds a mouse in her bed.
  (ii) Mary is hiding in the corner.
12(i) Mary paints a beautiful picture for the competition.
  (ii) Mary is dancing round the room.
13(i) John bumps into Mary.
  (ii) There is a puddle of milk on the floor.
14(i) John falls of his bike.
  (ii) John's leg is in plaster.
15(i) Mummy buys John an ice-cream.
  (ii) John is smiling.
16(i) Mary switches on the kettle.
  (ii) Steam is coming out of the kettle.

Appendix 5
Acceptability judgement
questionnaire based on Experiment 6

This questionnaire is designed to obtain adults' judgements about the acceptability of certain sentences. These judgements will help me to analyse the results of my research on children's language.

The items are based on a task in which the child is shown two pictures and these pictures are described to him. Then, he is asked to complete a sentence based on the pictures. For each item, please begin by reading the descriptions of the pictures (see page 10[1]). Then, read the corresponding set of sentences below. Your task is to rank the sentences for acceptability by placing a '1' beside the sentence which 'sounds best'; a '2' beside the sentence which 'sounds the next best'; and so on. If you think that two or more sentences are equally acceptable, then give them equal ranks by using an ' = ' sign (e.g. '2 = '). Please rank *all* the sentences in the set. If you think that any sentence is totally unacceptable, then place an asterisk beside it (as well as giving it a rank). Try not to spend too long thinking about any item. Please finish ranking each set of sentences before proceeding to the next set. Here is a summary of the ranking scale:

MOST ACCEPTABLE			LEAST ACCEPTABLE
('sounds best')			('sounds worst')

. . . .

1	2	3	4
' = ' = equally acceptable			'*' = totally unacceptable

	RANK
1. We can tell that Mary is sad because John broke her doll.	....
We can tell that Mary is sad because she is crying	....
Mary is sad because John broke her doll.	....
Mary is sad because she is crying.	....
2. Mummy gave John a row because he scribbled on the wallpaper.	....
Mummy gave John a row because he is crying.	....
We can tell that Mummy gave John a row because he scribbled on the wallpaper.	....
We can tell that Mummy gave John a row because he is crying.	....

[1]Page 10 of the questionnaire contained the descriptions of the pictures as shown in Appendix 4.

3. We can tell that the house is on fire because John dropped a match.   ....

   We can tell that the house is on fire because flames and smoke are coming out of it.   ....

   The house is on fire because flames and smoke are coming out of it.   ....

   The house is on fire because John dropped a match.   ....

4. The pillow burst because Mary is covered in feathers.   ....

   The pillow burst because Mary hit John with the pillow.   ....

   We can tell that the pillow burst because Mary is covered in feathers.   ....

   We can tell that the pillow burst because Mary hit John with the pillow.   ....

5. We can tell that Mary has a cold because she got soaked.   ....

   Mary has a cold because she is sneezing.   ....

   Mary has a cold because she got soaked.   ....

   We can tell that Mary has a cold because she is sneezing.   ....

6. Mary fell into the pond because she is dripping wet.   ....

   We can tell that Mary fell into the pond because she tripped over the cat.   ....

   We can tell that Mary fell into the pond because she is dripping wet.   ....

   Mary fell into the pond because she tripped over the cat.   ....

7. We can tell that John is cross because he is stamping his feet.   ....

   John is cross because Mary hid his car.   ....

   We can tell that John is cross because Mary hid his car.   ....

   John is cross because he is stamping his feet.   ....

8. Mummy told John he was a good boy because he washed up all the dishes.   ....

   Mummy told John he was a good boy because he is smiling.   ....

   We can tell that Mummy told John he was a good boy because he is smiling.   ....

   We can tell that Mummy told John he was a good boy because he washed up all the dishes.   ....

9. We can tell that the window broke because there is broken glass on the ground.   ....

   We can tell that the window broke because John threw a stone at it.   ....

   The window broke because there is broken glass on the ground.   ....

   The window broke because John threw a stone at it.   ....

10. We can tell that John shouted at Mary because Mary has her hands over her ears.   ....

    We can tell that John shouted at Mary because Mary tore John's book.   ....

    John shouted at Mary because Mary tore John's book.   ....

    John shouted at Mary because Mary has her hands over her ears.   ....

11. We can tell that Mary is scared because she found a mouse in her bed.   ....

Mary is scared because she found a mouse in her bed. ....

We can tell that Mary is scared because she is hiding in the corner. ....

Mary is scared because she is hiding in the corner. ....

12. Mary won a prize because she painted a beautiful picture for the competition. ....

We can tell that Mary won a prize because she is dancing round the room. ....

We can tell that Mary won a prize because she painted a beautiful picture for the competition. ....

Mary won a prize because she is dancing round the room. ....

13. Mary spilt the milk because John bumped into her. ....

We can tell that Mary spilt the milk because John bumped into her. ....

Mary spilt the milk because there is a puddle of milk on the floor. ....

We can tell that Mary spilt the milk because there is a puddle of milk on the floor. ....

14. John has a broken leg because he fell off his bike. ....

We can tell that John has a broken leg because his leg is in plaster. ....

John has a broken leg because his leg is in plaster. ....

We can tell that John has a broken leg because he fell off his bike. ....

15. We can tell that John is happy because Mummy bought him an ice-cream. ....

John is happy because Mummy bought him an ice-cream. ....

John is happy because he is smiling. ....

We can tell that John is happy because he is smiling. ....

16. We can tell that the kettle is boiling because steam is coming out of it. ....

The kettle is boiling because steam is coming out of it. ....

The kettle is boiling because Mary switched it on. ....

We can tell that the kettle is boiling because Mary switched it on. ....

Appendix 6
Materials used in Experiment 7
(Deductive Marking)

Sentence fragments used in sentence completion task

Sub-task A (sequential)

1. Snoopy has cream on his face so...
2. Charlie Brown has red paint on his hands so...
3. Donald Duck has muddy feet so...
4. Mickey Mouse has a necklace sticking out of his pocket so...

Sub-task B (simultaneous and causal)

5. There are footprints to the blue house so...
6. There is a light on in the red house so...
7. Charlie is crying so...
8. Charlie is smiling so...

Sub-task C (simultaneous and arbitrary/logical)

9. It's a red tin so...
10. It's a green tin so...
11. There's a horse inside so...
12. There's a pig inside so...

Descriptions of clues used in open-ended task

Sub-task A (sequential)

1. The clue is that Snoopy has cream on his face.
2. The clue is that Charlie Brown has red paint on his hands.
3. The clue is that Donald Duck has muddy feet.
4. The clue is that Mickey Mouse has a necklace sticking out of his pocket.

Sub-task B (simultaneous and causal)

5. The clue is that there are footprints to the blue house.
6. The clue is that there is a light on in the red house.
7. The clue is that Charlie is crying.
8. The clue is that Charlie is smiling.

Sub-task C (simultaneous and arbitrary/logical)

   9. The clue is that it's a red tin.
 10. The clue is that it's a green tin.
 11. The clue is that there's a horse inside.
 12. The clue is that there's a pig inside.

Notes

1. Introduction

1. The disadvantage of this strategy is that it might lead to false negatives if the children possessed the cognitive abilities but lacked the specifically linguistic knowledge which would enable them to use and understand the causal connectives appropriately. However, the strategy can be defended on the grounds that explaining is essentially a verbal activity. In any case this problem did not arise, since the children performed at a high level on the tasks.

2. This taxonomy may not be exhaustive. It might prove necessary to include additional categories, or to assign some phenomena to areas of overlap between two categories. Also, in the present study I shall be dealing only with particular subsets of the phenomena in each category. For example, all the physical phenomena involve observable events and no appeals are made to intervening variables.

3. In his discussion of converseness, Lyons is concerned with *logical* equivalence. As we shall see later (in section 4.1.2), *because* and *so* sentences are not equivalent in terms of their thematic structure.

4. The introduction of a CAUSE predicate has precedents both in the generative semanticists' work on causative verbs (e.g. McCawley, 1974), and in Miller and Johnson-Laird's work (1976) on procedural semantics.

5. The claim that *because* and *so* convey temporal order information is much more debatable when the explanation is in the intentional or deductive mode rather than the empirical mode. (See sections 5.1.3 and 6.1.4.)

6. This distinction between primary and secondary functions owes much to Karmiloff-Smith's distinction (1979) between primary and secondary focussing functions. However, there is a certain amount of ambiguity in Karmiloff-Smith's account as to whether these functions are to be regarded as intrinsic properties of particular words, or as characterisations of the way speakers use the words on particular occasions. Thus, it is not totally clear whether a word's primary focussing function is fixed or variable. The former interpretation (intrinsic property of word/fixed) seems more useful for present purposes, and this is the sense in which I shall use 'primary function' and 'secondary function'.

7. An explanation of this apparent paradox is given in section 4.1.4.

2. The development of the causal connectives and of causality

1. Piaget did present an oral version of the task to a smaller group of 6- to 10-year-olds, but he reports neither the details of the items nor the details of the results.
2. This assumption is closely related to Grice's maxim of quality (Grice, 1975).
3. Flores d'Arcais did include some 'filler' items which consisted of synonymous sentences, but he does not give any details of these items.
4. This task could be regarded either as a comprehension task or as a production task. It has been included in the comprehension category because it is the experimenter rather than the child who produces the causal connective.
5. I was not aware of this study until after I had designed and carried out the studies reported in this book.
6. This study is also reported in Hood and Bloom (1979).

3. Elicited production studies

1. The story-telling task used in this experiment is an 'inverse' version of a task used by Light (1979) in which the child was presented with a story and was asked to select a facial expression to match the story. Both Light's task and the present task employ the same four emotional categories, but the schematic faces used in the two studies are not identical.
2. It was hoped that the delay would result in the author forgetting the connectives which had appeared in the original transcripts. Of course, even if the actual connectives were forgotten, it would still be possible for the connectives to influence the coding indirectly. The connectives might have affected the author's initial interpretation of the relations, and this initial interpretation might have been remembered even when the connectives were forgotten. Nevertheless, it is likely that this procedure at least reduced the influence of the connectives on the coding.
3. This type of response may have been encouraged by the experimenter's script, which included such comments as 'I don't want the marbles to fall down and make a loud noise.' (See Appendix 1.)

4. The empirical mode

1. All the sequences except sequence (8) (see Appendix 2) were acted out in both orders. The normal order of sequence (8) (Coco pushes the cup → the cup falls → the cup breaks) was acted out and video-taped. For the reversed order, the events were acted out and video-taped in the following way:
   (a) Coco pushes the cup (to the edge of the table)
   (b) the cup falls → the cup breaks. (The cup was made to fall by pulling it with thread which was not visible on the video-tape, rather than by Coco pushing it.)

Then the desired sequence was obtained by editing the video-tape.

5. The intentional mode

1. For convenience, 'result' will be used to refer to the event/state which the agent intends to bring about irrespective of whether the relation between the action and this event/state is causal or conditional.
2. I shall leave open the question of whether this is an instance of polysemy or of homonymy. While this question is of considerable interest from the point of view of theoretical linguistics, it is not directly relevant to my present concern.
3. In the sentence completion task, the children sometimes used a connective other than the one at the end of the sentence fragment, for example:

   E: *Mary put on a pretty dress so...*
   S: *Because she was going to Anne's party.*

   These responses were coded twice: once on the basis of the original connective and once on the basis of the connective used by the subject. The results presented in Table 25 are based on the connective used by the subject. However, equally striking results are obtained when the analysis is based on the original connective.

6. The deductive mode

1. I am using the term 'deductive' in its common usage sense of 'derived as a conclusion from something already known or assumed' (*Oxford English Dictionary*), rather than in the narrower sense which it has in logic where is contrasts with 'inductive'. Thus, sentences in the deductive mode are not necessarily based on logical inferences and do not necessarily involve reasoning from the general to the particular.
2. Piaget's distinction between justification and explanation is similar to my distinction between the deductive and empirical modes.
3. There are two points which should be noted regarding the prior/future/simultaneous distinction. First, this distinction is relevant only when the content is physical or psychological. Deductive sentences which have logical content can only be in the simultaneous category. Second, the prior/future/simultaneous distinction is not absolutely clear-cut. For example, it is likely that John's leg was broken for some time before it was in plaster so the two states are not strictly simultaneous. Conversely, as with many causal sequences, it is not possible to draw a sharp dividing line between the event of Mary spilling the milk and the state of there being a puddle on the floor. However, the degree of temporal overlap between the events/states is considerably greater for 'simultaneous' sentences than for 'prior' or 'future' sentences.
4. The analysis was based on the responses the children gave when they were asked to produce the whole sentence. This is because some of the children produced the whole sentence as soon as the experimenter had given the sentence fragment, rather than completing the fragment first. Therefore, all the children gave a 'whole sentence' response to all the items, whereas the 'completion' data are incomplete. In most cases, where both types of response were given, they were fairly similar to one another.

References

Bebout, L. J., Segalowitz, S. J. and White, G. J. 1980. Children's comprehension of causal constructions with because and so. *Child Development* 51, 565–8

Berzonsky, M. D. 1971. The role of familiarity in children's explanations of physical causality. *Child Development* 42, 705–15

Bever, T. G. 1970. The cognitive basis for linguistic structures. In J. R. Hayes (ed.), *Cognition and the Development of Language*. New York: Wiley

Bloom, L. 1974. Talking, understanding and thinking. In R. L. Schiefelbusch and L. L. Lloyd (eds.), *Language Perspectives: Acquisition, Retardation and Intervention*. London: Macmillan

Bloom, L., Lahey, M., Hood, L., Lifter, K. and Fiess, K. 1980. Complex sentences: acquisition of syntactic connectives and the semantic relations they encode. *Journal of Child Language* 7, 235–61

Bullock, M. 1984. Preschool children's understanding of causal connections. *British Journal of Developmental Psychology* 2, 139–48

Bullock, M. and Gelman, R. 1979. Preschool children's assumptions about cause and effect: temporal ordering. *Child Development* 50, 89–96

Campbell, R. N., Macdonald, T. B. and Dockrell, J. E. 1982. The relationship between comprehension and production and its ontogenesis. In F. Lowenthal, F. Vandamme and J. Cordier (eds.) *Language and Language Acquisition*. New York: Plenum

Chapman, R. S. and Miller, J. F. 1975. Word order in early two and three word utterances: does production precede comprehension? *Journal of Speech and Hearing Research* 18, 355–71

Clancy, P., Jacobsen, T. and Silva, M. 1976. The acquisition of conjunction: a cross-linguistic study. *Stanford Papers and Reports on Child Language Development* 12, 71–80

Clark, E. V. 1971. On the acquisition of the meaning of 'before' and 'after'. *Journal of Verbal Learning and Verbal Behavior* 10, 266–75

1973. How children describe time and order. In C. A. Ferguson and D. I. Slobin (eds.), *Studies of Child Language Development*. New York: Holt, Rinehart and Winston

Clark, E. V. and Hecht, B. F. 1982. Learning to coin agent and instrument nouns. *Cognition* 12, 1–24

1983. Comprehension, production, and language acquisition. *Annual Review of Psychology* 34, 325–49

Clark, R., Hutcheson, S. and Van Buren, P. 1974. Comprehension and production in language acquisition. *Journal of Linguistics* 10, 39–54

Connell, P. J. and McReynolds, L. V. 1981. An experimental analysis of children's generalization during lexical learning: comprehension or production. *Applied Psycholinguistics 2*, 309–32

Corrigan, R. 1975. A scalogram analysis of the development of the use and comprehension of 'because' in children. *Child Development 46*, 195–201

Cromer, R. 1978. The strengths of the weak form of the cognition hypothesis for language acquisition. In V. Lee (ed.), *Language Development*. London: Croom Helm

Deutsche, J. M. 1937. *The Development of Children's Concepts of Causal Relations*. Minneapolis: University of Minnesota Press

Donaldson, M. 1978. *Children's Minds*. London: Fontana

Donaldson, M. L. 1980. The case of the disappearing train: is it coming or going? A study of children's and adults' use of some deictic verbs. Unpublished MA thesis, University of Edinburgh

Emerson, H. F. 1979. Children's comprehension of 'because' in reversible and non-reversible sentences. *Journal of Child Language 6*, 279–300

Emerson, H. F. and Gekoski, W. L. 1980. Development of comprehension of sentences with 'because' or 'if'. *Journal of Experimental Child Psychology 29*, 202–24

Epstein, H. L. 1972. The child's understanding of causal connectives. Unpublished PhD thesis, University of Wisconsin

Evans, J. St B. T., Barston, J. L. and Pollard, P. 1983. On the conflict between logic and belief in syllogistic reasoning. *Memory and Cognition 11*, 295–306

Flavell, J., Botkin, P., Fry, C., Wright, J. and Jarvis, P. 1968. *The Development of Role-taking and Communication Skills in Children*. New York: Wiley

Flores d'Arcais, G. B. 1978a. The acquisition of the subordinating constructions in children's language. In R. N. Campbell and P. T. Smith (eds.), *Recent Advances in the Psychology of Language*, vol. 4A. London: Plenum

1978b. Levels of semantic knowledge in children's use of connectives. In A. Sinclair, R. J. Jarvella and W. J. M. Levelt (eds.), *The Child's Conception of Language*. Berlin: Springer-Verlag

Gleitman, L. R., Gleitman, H. and Shipley, E. F. 1972. The emergence of the child as grammarian. *Cognition 1*, 137–64

Gopnik, A. 1984. The acquisition of 'gone' and the development of the object concept. *Journal of Child Language 11*, 273–92

Grice, H. P. 1975. Logic and conversation. In P. Cole and J. L. Morgan (eds.), *Syntax and Semantics, Vol. 3: Speech Acts*. London: Academic Press

Hagtvet, B. E. 1982. On the relation between language comprehension and language production in a social psychological perspective. In F. Lowenthal, F. Vandamme and J. Cordier (eds.), *Language and Language Acquisition*. New York: Plenum

Hoenigmann-Stovall, N. M. 1982. Extralinguistic control of language comprehension and production in the nonfluent child. *Journal of Psycholinguistic Research 11*, 1–17

Hood, L. 1977. A longitudinal study of the development of the expression of causal relations in complex sentences. Unpublished PhD thesis, Columbia University

Hood, L. and Bloom, L. 1979. What, when and how about why: a longitudinal study of early expressions of causality. *Monographs of the Society for Research in Child Development*, vol. 44, no. 6

Huang, I. 1943. Children's conception of physical causality: a critical summary. *Journal of Genetic Psychology 63*, 71–121

Huang, I., Yang, H. C. and Yao, F. Y. 1945. Principles of selection in children's 'phenomenistic' explanations. *Journal of Genetic Psychology 66*, 63–8

References

Johnson, H. L. and Chapman, R. S. 1980. Children's judgement and recall of causal connectives: a developmental study of 'because', 'so', and 'and'. *Journal of Psycholinguistic Research 9*, 243–60

Johnson-Laird, P. N. 1983. *Mental Models*. Cambridge University Press

Karmiloff-Smith, A. 1979. *A Functional Approach to Child Language*. Cambridge University Press

Karniol, R. 1978. Children's use of intention cues in evaluating behaviour. *Psychological Bulletin 85*, 76–85

Katz, E. W. and Brent, S. B. 1968. Understanding connectives. *Journal of Verbal Learning and Verbal Behaviour 7*, 501–9

Keil, F. 1979. The development of the young child's ability to anticipate the outcomes of simple causal events. *Child Development 50*, 455–62

Kuhn, D. and Phelps, H. 1976. The development of children's comprehension of causal direction. *Child Development 47*, 248–51

Kun, A. 1978. Evidence for preschoolers' understanding of causal direction in extended causal sequences. *Child Development 49*, 218–22

Laurendeau, M. and Pinard, A. 1962. *Causal Thinking in Children*. New York: International Universities Press

Leslie, A. M. 1982. The perception of causality in infants. *Perception 11*, 173–86
   1984. Infant perception of a manual pick-up event. *British Journal of Developmental Psychology 2*, 19–32

Light, P. 1979. *The Development of Social Sensitivity*. Cambridge University Press

Limber, J. 1973. The genesis of complex sentences. In T. E. Moore (ed.), *Cognitive Development and the Acquisition of Language*. London: Academic Press

Lyons, J. 1977. *Semantics*. Cambridge University Press

McCabe, A. and Peterson, C. 1985. A naturalistic study of the production of causal connectives by children. *Journal of Child Language 12*, 145–59

McCawley, J. D. 1974. Prelexical syntax. In P. A. M. Seuren (ed.), *Semantic Syntax*. Oxford University Press

Mendelson, R. and Shultz, T. R. 1976. Covariation and temporal contiguity as principles of causal inference in young children. *Journal of Experimental Child Psychology 22*, 408–12

Miller, G. A. and Johnson-Laird, P. N. 1976. *Language and Perception*. Cambridge University Press

Moran, J. D. III and McCullers, J. C. 1984. The effects of recency and story content on children's moral judgments. *Journal of Experimental Child Psychology 38*, 447–55

Piaget, J. 1926. *The Language and Thought of the Child*. London: Routledge and Kegan Paul
   1928. *Judgement and Reasoning in the Child*. London: Routledge and Kegan Paul
   1929. *The Child's Conception of the World*. London: Routledge and Kegan Paul
   1930. *The Child's Conception of Causality*. Totowa, NJ: Littlefield, Adams
   1976. *The Grasp of Consciousness*. Cambridge, Mass.: Harvard University Press
   1978. *Success and Understanding*. London: Routledge and Kegan Paul

Reid, J. F. 1983. Into print: reading and language growth. In M. Donaldson, R. Grieve and C. Pratt (eds.), *Early Childhood Development and Education*. Oxford: Blackwell

Roth, P. L. 1980. The development of the child's use of causal language to infer physical and psychological causation. Unpublished PhD thesis, University of Wisconsin

Searle, J. R. 1981. The intentionality of intention and action. In D. A. Norman (ed.), *Perspectives on Cognitive Science*. London: Lawrence Erlbaum

Sedlak, A. J. and Kurtz, S. T. 1981. A review of children's use of causal inference principles. *Child Development 52*, 759–84

Shultz, T. R. 1980. Development of the concept of intention. In W. A. Collins (ed.), *The Minnesota Symposia on Child Psychology*, vol. 13. Hillsdale, NJ: Lawrence Erlbaum

   1982. Causal reasoning in the social and nonsocial realms. *Canadian Journal of Behavioural Science 14*, 307–22

Shultz, T. R. and Mendelson, R. 1975. The use of covariation as a principle of causal analysis. *Child Development 46*, 394–9

Shultz, T. R. and Ravinsky, F. B. 1977. Similarity as a principle of causal inference. *Child Development 48*, 1552–8

Siegler, R. S. 1975. Defining the locus of developmental differences in children's causal reasoning. *Journal of Experimental Child Psychology 20*, 512–25

   1976. The effects of simple necessity and sufficiency relationships on children's causal inferences. *Child Development 47*, 1058–63

Siegler, R. S. and Liebert, R. M. 1974. Effects of contiguity, regularity, and age on children's causal inferences. *Developmental Psychology 10*, 574–9

Sinclair, A., Jarvella, R. J. and Levelt, W. J. M. (eds.) 1978. *The Child's Conception of Language*. Berlin: Springer-Verlag

Sophian, C. and Huber, A. 1984. Early developments in children's causal judgments. *Child Development 55*, 512–26

Stein, N. L. and Trabasso, T. 1982. Children's understanding of stories: a basis for moral judgment and dilemma resolution. In C. J. Brainerd and M. Pressley (eds.), *Verbal Processes in Children*. New York: Springer-Verlag

Straight, H. S. 1982. Structural commonalities between comprehension and production products of monitoring and anticipation. In F. Lowenthal, F. Vandamme and J Cordier (eds.), *Language and Language Acquisition*. New York: Plenum

Sullivan, L. 1972. Development of causal connectives by children. *Perceptual and Motor Skills 35*, 1003–10

Tager-Flusberg, H. 1981. Sentence comprehension in autistic children. *Applied Psycholinguistics 2*, 5–24

Trabasso, T., Stein, N. L. and Johnson, L. R. 1981. Children's knowledge of events: a causal analysis of story structure. In G. H. Bower (ed.), *The Psychology of Learning and Motivation*, vol. 15. New York: Academic Press

Werner, H. and Kaplan, B. 1963. *Symbol Formation*. New York: Wiley

Winitz, H., Sanders, R. and Kort, J. 1981. Comprehension and production of the /-əz/ plural allomorph. *Journal of Psycholinguistic Research 10*, 259–71

Yuill, N. 1984. Young children's coordination of motive and outcome in judgements of satisfaction and morality. *British Journal of Developmental Psychology 2*, 73–81

Index

Index